Vanishing Cultures of
SOUTH
AFRICA

Dedicated to the Ndimande family

Vanishing Cultures of
SOUTH AFRICA

Changing customs in a changing world

PETER MAGUBANE

RIZZOLI
NEW YORK

First published in the United States of America in 1998 by
RIZZOLI INTERNATIONAL PUBLICATIONS, INC.
300 Park Avenue South, New York, NY 10010

First published in Great Britain in 1998 by New Holland (Publishers) Ltd
London • Cape Town • Sydney • Singapore

Library of Congress Cataloging-in-Publication Data

Magubane, Peter.
Vanishing cultures of South Africa / Peter Magubane, Alan Mountain.
p.   cm.
Includes index.
ISBN 0-8478-2097-1 (hardcover)
1. Ethnology—South Africa. 2. South Africa—Civilization.
3. South Africa—Social life and customs. I. Mountain, Alan.
II. Title.
CN656.M34   1998
306'.0968—dc21   97–46829
                                                  CIP

Managing editor: Annlerie van Rooyen
Designer: Janice Evans
Editor: Lesley Hay-Whitton
Design assistant: Lellyn Creamer
Cartographer: Desireé Oosterberg
Indexer: Glynne Newlands
Proofreader: Tessa Kennedy

Reproduction by Hirt & Carter Cape (Pty) Ltd
Printed and bound by Tien Wah Press (Pte.) Ltd, Singapore

ACKNOWLEDGEMENTS
I acknowledge the enormous contribution made by the Goodman Gallery, who supported me throughout
this project. I would also like to acknowledge support received from the Chairman's Fund, without which
this project would not have been a success. Lastly, I would like to acknowledge Cindy Futhane's
tireless efforts with captions and explanations of concepts, from Sesotho and Ndebele to Zulu.
PETER MAGUBANE
JOHANNESBURG, 1998

FRONT COVER: A male Xhosa initiate in the initiation lodge where they are secluded.
BACK COVER: An Ndebele woman wearing the older, permanent neck ring.
COVER SPINE: An example of the beadwork worn at the Zulu Reed Ceremony.
PAGE 1: A female Basotho initiate.
PAGES 2 AND 3: Male Ntwana initiates bow their heads as a sign of deference.

CONTENTS

Nelson Mandela five days after his release from prison.

Tuynhuys
Private Bag X1000
Cape Town 8000
Tel: (021) 45-2225

South Africa is proud of its diverse cultural wealth and traditions. Although some cultural traditions have been forsaken, others still form an integral part of our daily life, often blending with each other and with modern elements to present a fascinating juxtaposition of old and new.

Peter Magubane, who has made an outstanding contribution to photo-journalism over the past four decades, has utilised his talents as a photographer to capture this national treasure of our society and record it for posterity.

I am honoured to have this opportunity to make a humble contribution to creative endeavour.

NELSON MANDELA
President
Republic of South Africa

INTRODUCTION

ndigenous African culture, in common with other cultures, has always been dynamic, adapting itself to external circumstances and events. In *Vanishing Cultures of South Africa* we have painted a broad overview of the indigenous South African cultures as photographed by Peter Magubane over a period of several years. The photographs underscore the inevitability of social and cultural change, providing graphic evidence of vibrant transformation.

In the course of the 19th and 20th centuries, many changes have been wrought through the impact of Christianity on indigenous religious practices, the growth of the migrant labour system, the gradual transformation of rural into urban communities, as well as responses to the realities of modern consumerism. In the process, much has been lost for ever, including various forms of dress and rituals that are associated with the investiture of traditional leaders.

Yet there has also been a resurgence of certain rituals like initiation practices since the 1970s, when the rise of the black consciousness movement encouraged people to embrace the values of earlier generations. In some cases, new ceremonies were introduced in a deliberate attempt to revive people's pride in their cultural heritage. Among these are the annual Shaka Day celebrations organized to coincide with the anniversary of the death of the first king of the Zulu empire, Shaka.

Even though the rituals people observe today sometimes bear little, if any, resemblance to the practices of their 19th century predecessors, many of them still regard themselves as traditionalists. Like successive earlier generations, they often lay claim to the idea of continuity, despite the inevitability of change. Viewed from this perspective, all so-called traditional communities are in a state of flux, constantly confronted with the choice either of renewing their connection to the past, or of embracing a new, and ultimately different, future. This can be said not only of the large polities that first emerged in southern Africa in the early 19th century, but also of their Iron Age forebears.

The peopling of southern Africa has been the subject of an ongoing debate between researchers relying on archaeological, linguistic and oral evidence. Archaeology tells us when and where people settled, more or less how they lived, what they ate and so on. It can also link groups together through the artefacts they left behind (e.g. pottery). Linguistics, through the study of cognate languages and morphology, tells us how people related to one another. Reliance on oral traditions becomes increasingly problematic the further back one delves into the past, particularly when there is no corroborative archaeological and linguistic evidence. Historians nevertheless agree that oral traditions are not the product of sheer invention.

Archaeologists have discovered early traces of human occupation at Sterkfontein Caves in the province of Gauteng, where the perfectly preserved skull of 'Mrs. Ples', a female hominid specimen, dating back some two and a half million years, was found in 1947. To date some 600 hominid specimens have been found, which makes Sterkfontein the richest *Australopithecus* site in Africa. The oldest tools used in southern Africa, from the Early Stone Age, were also found at Sterkfontein, dating back some 1.6 million years.

Because the terms Early Stone Age, Middle Stone Age and Later Stone Age have both cultural and chronological connotations, archaeologists have become increasingly reluctant to apply them. These terms nevertheless remain convenient labels. It is therefore still common to refer to the period between the first appearance of stone artefacts and the disappearance of large cutting tools such as hand axes and cleavers as the Early Iron Age. This period is divided into the Oldowan era, the most ancient, and the later Acheulian era, which comprises the majority of Early Stone Age sites found in South Africa, and which lasted for more than a million years.

The Middle Stone Age, which began around 200,000 BP (Before Present) and terminated around 30,000 BP, is characterized by the use of flake and blade tools such as points and scrapers. Grindstones, although relatively rare in Middle Stone Age assemblages, probably reflect regional differences in the processing of plant foods. Most of these stones have been found in the Gauteng area, where above-ground food plants like seeds and nuts are comparatively common. Some communities also hunted docile animals like the eland, while the occupants of coastal caves ate sea birds and marine animals.

The Later Stone Age has continued through to the present day in certain isolated and remote areas of Namibia and Botswana, where some members of the San community still live as hunter-gatherers even though they no longer rely on the use of stone tools. Archaeological research has established that somewhere between 7,000 and 2,000 BP a considerable number of changes took place in the hunter-gatherer economies of the Later Stone Age people of South Africa, as a greater variety of foodstuffs was sought and more sophisticated tools and

Top: A painting by 18th-century French traveller François Le Vaillant, depicting a hunter from the region now known as the Northern Cape. Le Vaillant called the group to which the man in this painting belonged the 'Housouana', thought to be San (or Bushmen); he claimed that the whisk in the man's hand was to wipe sweat away.

artefacts were constructed. New technologies, such as the bow and arrow and various traps and snares, increased the access of Later Stone Age hunters to the local game population and enabled them to deal more effectively with potentially dangerous animals like wild pigs.

The influx first of Iron Age agriculturalists and later of European farmers made it increasingly difficult for these communities to maintain their nomadic lifestyles. Available evidence nevertheless indicates that, for more than a millennium, Stone and Iron Age communities were able to coexist, mainly because the hunter-gathers did not compete with the pastoralists for resources like grazing and the land needed to cultivate grains. Indeed there was a certain amount of intermarriage, and cultural and linguistic assimilation.

Archaeologists have determined that Early Iron Age communities were already resident in South Africa by AD 200. It is even possible that grain farming may have been established shortly before the Christian era, leading communities to build permanent settlements. These newly settled communities needed iron for hoes, and also axes to cut and burn clearings for fields. The development of this new technology included the production of decorated pots and bowls for preparing and storing food. In some cases, ornate metalwork and complex terracotta sculptures were also manufactured. Notable in this regard are the Lydenburg

LEGEND

Ndebele
Pedi
Zulu
Tsonga
Basotho
Tswana
Xhosa
Venda
Ntwana

The Kalahari San have not been shown due to their nomadic lifestyle.

heads found at a 5th-century site in Mpumalanga. The subsequent addition of cattle and other domestic animals led gradually to the introduction of farming patterns that are still widely practised today.

Both pottery remains and settlement patterns have been used to study these pre-colonial communities, in the latter case by plotting variations in architectural styles with the aid of aerial photographs. Initially, however, archaeologists relied mainly on the colour, texture and finish of pottery fragments to identify particular traditions and to determine the ways in which different styles spread across the subcontinent. Following the development of radiocarbon dating in the 1950s, the time sequences ascribed to some of these Iron Age pottery styles were revised. The issue of whether or not it is possible to discern continuities in pottery styles from the Early to the Late Iron Age nevertheless has continued to inform the debate on the evidence afforded by remains of this kind.

Most archaeologists agree that the earliest Iron Age phase in the subcontinent is provided by the Matola tradition, which is believed to have spread southwards through the coastlands of southern Africa. This tradition, which is named after the site in Mozambique where the Matola pottery style was first found, suggests that migration probably took place down the continent's eastern seaboard, penetrating as far south as present-day Scottburgh. What happened subsequently is less clear. Some archaeologists favour the idea of local continuity, arguing that Matola-style ceramics from sites such as Mzonjani developed into Lydenburg-style pottery at sites such as Ndondondwane. In contrast to these researchers, others claim that there is no relationship between the Lydenburg and the Matola traditions. According to them, the Lydenburg tradition originated in a separate, later migration down the south-east coast of Africa. Thus, despite the fact that archaeologists no longer question the chronologies developed through radiocarbon dating, there is very little agreement among them on how to interpret these Iron Age ceramic sequences.

Most Iron Age communities produced, on a limited scale, metal implements that were made from locally available low-grade ore. However, there is also evidence to suggest that some villages produced iron in excess of their needs. This led to greater economic specialization, as these communities began to make part of their living by bartering with others. The earliest indication of overseas trade relations dates to the 9th century, when local Iron Age communities started exchanging ivory and gold for beads and cloth. The desire to control this external trade led ultimately to the formation of large, hierarchically structured groups.

It is from these Iron Age communities that today's Bantu-speaking peoples emerged, of whom more than 90 percent are accounted for by two large language groupings: the Nguni-speaking communities who settled mainly along the eastern seaboard and adjacent hinterland, and the Sotho-Tswana people who settled on the central highland plateau. The balance of South Africa's Bantu-speaking communities are accounted for by two groups, the Venda and the Tsonga ('Shangaan').

There are a variable number of linguistically and culturally distinct groups within the broad divisions of Nguni-speaking and Sotho-Tswana peoples. Historically, the groups formed by the members of these linguistic groups were based on affiliation to an hereditary chief who had jurisdiction over a defined area. This pattern of authority, which was established long before the region was colonized by European settlers, is still recognized today, even though continuity between past and present practices is increasingly threatened by rural women's demands for equal access to land and other resources.

Nguni-speakers account for about 60 percent of the Bantu-speaking peoples of South Africa. Before the advent of rapid urbanization, they lived mostly along the eastern seaboard and adjacent inland areas, reaching up to the escarpment which divides the coastal lowlands from the central highlands. However, there is a small offshoot of the Nguni-speaking people, the Ndebele, who make up some two and a half percent of South Africa's Bantu-speaking peoples. In the 19th century, this group settled among the Sotho people who were living on the Highveld in the present-day province of Mpumalanga. Nguni-speakers living along the seaboard are divided into three broad divisions based on linguistic and cultural differences.

Those located in the present-day Eastern Cape, between the Fish River in the south and the umThamvuna River in the north, and from the sea to the southern Drakensberg Escarpment, speak closely related dialects and are collectively referred to as Xhosa, the dominant language in the area. There are nine Xhosa-speaking groups, the chiefs of which are related to, but politically independent from one another: the Xhosa, Thembu, Mpondo, Mpondomise, Bomvana, Xesibe, Mfengu, Bhaca and Ntlangwini. While some of these chiefdom clusters are much larger than others, there is considerable cultural conformity among them. This conformity is reflected in, for example, the layout of homesteads and the prevalence, even today, of initiation practices organized at a local rather than chiefly level.

Between the umThamvuna River in the extreme south of present-day KwaZulu-Natal and the Phongola River in the north are the Zulu-speakers, who are slightly more numerous than their Xhosa-speaking neighbours. Prior to the rise of the Zulu empire at the beginning of the 19th century, each of the hundreds of small groups in this region was autonomous but, with Shaka's accession to power, they were either incorporated into the Zulu kingdom, or forced into tributary relations.

North of the Zulu are the Swazi, of whom the majority (approximately 60 percent) are resident in Swaziland today. For this reason, they have been omitted from this book. Like their Zulu-speaking neighbours, the Swazi continue to practise ceremonies, some of which date to the 19th century and earlier.

The Sotho-Tswana division, resident throughout much of central South Africa and neighbouring areas, such as Lesotho and Botswana, accounts for a little over one third of South Africa's Bantu-speaking peoples. Besides the differences in language, another important distinguishing feature of the Sotho-Tswana is the use of totems to trace patrilineal descent from a common putative ancestor (or totem). Generally speaking, the totem (or identifying emblem) is an animal that is never hunted or exploited in any way. The Sotho-Tswana are divided into three broad subgroups: the Southern Sotho (Basotho), the Western Sotho (Tswana), and the Northern Sotho (Pedi).

The Southern Sotho, who call themselves Basotho, comprise about 17 percent of southern Africa's Bantu-speaking peoples. The Basotho display a high level of homogeneity, despite their disparate origins. This

ABOVE: *The homestead of the 19th-century Ngqika (Xhosa) chief Sandile, as depicted by Thomas Baines, who can himself just be seen on the extreme left of the painting. The standing figure in the centre of the painting is thought to be Sandile. In 1846 one of Sandile's people stole an axe from a shop in Fort Beaufort; when Sandile refused to hand over the culprit to the authorities, the Seventh Frontier War (or the War of the Axe) broke out.*

came about during the highly disruptive period of the Lifaqane (Mfecane), when the far-sighted leader of the Kwena (crocodile) totemic cluster, Moshoeshoe, brought together the scattered Sotho-Tswana remnants of Nguni raids, who were living at the time in appalling conditions around the Butha Buthe district of present-day Lesotho, and melded them into a single, Basotho, nation.

The Western Sotho, or Tswana, constitute about 10 percent of southern Africa's Bantu-speaking people. The largest Western Sotho groupings are the Tlhaping, whose totem is a fish; the Rolong (iron); the Hurutshe who broke away from the Rolong; the Kwena; and the Kgatla (monkey).

The Northern Sotho are linguistically and culturally the most diverse of all the Sotho-Tswana groups, today comprising some 136 separate chiefdoms, including the little-studied Ntwana. The most prominent group within the Northern Sotho is the Pedi who, in the course of the 18th century, created a powerful empire that extended from the Limpopo River in the north to the Vaal River in the south. Although the Pedi eventually lost much of their control across most of that area, the kingdom today nevertheless remains an important confederation of semi-autonomous chiefdoms under the Sekhukhune leaders.

The Venda comprise an independent group of polities who live in and around the Soutpansberg Mountains in the Northern Province. They make up only 2 percent of the total Bantu-speaking peoples in South Africa and are of varying origins. The greater part of the population, the Thavatsindi and the Singo, originated in the Shona areas of Zimbabwe, while a smaller group, the Ngona, claims descent from the early inhabitants of the Soutpansberg.

The Tsonga, located in eastern Mpumalanga, comprise a cultural and linguistic amalgam of coastal Nguni-speakers, who migrated into the area following the defeat of the Ndwandwe polity by Shaka early in the 19th century, and local Tsonga-speaking people whose cultural nucleus lies in Mozambique.

THE XHOSA

The Xhosa-speaking peoples or Cape Nguni inhabit the Eastern Cape, from the

KwaZulu-Natal border to the Eastern Cape Zuurveld. Historically they were hunters,

herders and subsistence farmers, who were organized in more or less politically

independent chiefdom clusters, each recognizing a paramount chief. Xhosa,

like Nguni, a linguistic rather than an ethnic term, was the dialect spoken in

the valleys of the Fish, Keiskamma and Buffalo rivers.

Historical evidence suggests that as early as 1593 there were Xhosa-speaking people as far south as the Umthatha River in the area known today as the Eastern Cape, and that they had probably already been in the region for some time prior to that. According to oral tradition, Thembu, Xhosa and Mpondomise peoples had inhabited the upper reaches of the Eastern Cape Umzimvubu River for generations before they came down to the coast. All of this suggests that scholarly speculations about the migration of Xhosa-speaking people from East Africa in the distant past are unfounded, if not misguided or something rather more sinister. Archaeological research, among other things, will undoubtedly cast more light on such questions in future. For example, excavations recently undertaken on the farm Canasta Place near present-day East London suggest that, since the 7th century AD, Xhosa-speaking people had been living more or less continuously near the Buffalo River.

During the 19th century Hlubi, Zizi, Tolo and Bhele peoples migrated into the region that later came to be called Transkei (now part of the Eastern Cape). These people, who subsequently became known as the Mfengu, were dependants of the Xhosa Paramount Chief Hintsa. In 1835 they were claimed by the missionaries and the British colonial authorities as 'refugees from the Mfecane', i.e. the Zulu King Shaka's 'total war' of the late 1820s (*see page 34*). They were brought under colonial protection primarily in order to swell depleted labour reserves. The Mfengu were military collaborators of the whites against the Xhosa in the Frontier Wars of 1846–7, 1850–3 and 1877–8. As a consequence of their efforts in defence of the Cape Colony, the Mfengu obtained from the white authorities grants of land which formerly belonged to the Xhosa.

In the growing confrontation on the frontier and the successive clashes with British and colonial troops, Xhosa chiefs, among them Sandile and Maqoma, emerged as patriots who were fighting to retain their independence, lands and followers. Maqoma, a gifted strategist

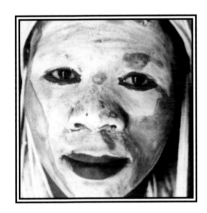

and hardy guerrilla fighter, died a prisoner on Robben Island in 1873. Sandile was mortally wounded in a skirmish with Mfengu conscripts in the Isidenge Forest in May 1878. With their passing so, too, the last remnants of Xhosa military resistance to colonial rule crumbled. In the early 1880s the Mpondo were the last of the Cape Nguni chiefdoms to be brought under colonial rule.

The Xhosa on the Eastern Cape frontier were the first Cape Nguni chiefdom who were exposed to European explorers, hunters, traders, missionaries, soldiers and colonial administrators on an ever-increasing scale from the late 18th century onwards. These cross-cultural contacts were to have profound effects on Cape Nguni culture which, to some extent, are still discernible to this day. Ntsikana, a famous Xhosa prophet who died in 1821, was a convert of the Reverend Joseph Williams of the London Missionary Society. Although he was an illiterate man, Ntsikana composed hymns, which are still sung by modern-day Christian congregations. In addition, he made fascinating prophecies, warning of the growing importance of 'buttons without holes' (money) and foretelling of 'snakes belching fire' (trains) which would move over the countryside.

Conversion to Christianity resulted in the development of a major cleavage in Cape Nguni society, which was to last up until the 1950s, between the so-called 'School' people and 'Red' traditionalists. The former, who embraced Christianity and Western education, were essentially the product of the mission stations and schools. They

TOP AND OPPOSITE: *After they have undergone circumcision, Xhosa male initiates* (abakhwetha) *are secluded in the bush in temporary shelters. At this stage, they rub white clay* (ifutha) *on their faces and bodies. While in seclusion, the initiates must abstain* (ukuzila) *from meat, sour milk, tobacco, liquor and sexual intercourse, and they are considered to be 'in the care of the ancestors'.*

OPPOSITE, TOP: Initiates (abakhwetha) in their makeshift shelter, a week before they return to society as men. OPPOSITE, BOTTOM, AND ABOVE: During their period in seclusion, the initiates practise the traditional art of stick-fighting to establish the local champion. He would compete with the victors from other areas at a later stage, to establish the overall champion. PAGES 16 AND 17: In a departure from the norm, a white university student, who has probably grown up among the Xhosa and assimilated their culture, takes part in the initiation proceedings. At the end of the period in seclusion, the initiates run down to the river, where they wash the white clay off their bodies. Afterwards, they smear themselves with fat or butter (amafutha). They are then covered with new blankets and presented with sticks (iminqayi), which have been blackened in the fire. The iminqayi symbolize peace and the initiates' newly acquired ability to settle disputes within the group with words rather than resorting to blows. Today, adult men still carry the black stick or rod (umnqayi) when consulting a diviner or herbalist. The initiates are now ready to be reincorporated into routine social life as young men who are eligible to marry.

were greatly influenced by contemporary European, particularly English-speaking, culture, as imparted to them in word and deed by the missionaries. The 'School' people adopted a distinctive style of dress and evolved cultural traditions which centred on church and school. Traditionalists were described as 'Red' because of their practice of smearing red clay on their faces and bodies. Rejecting both the church and Western education as foreign introductions, the traditionalists continued to perform time-honoured rituals centring around the spirits of the ancestors (see page 28).

Xhosa-speakers are today predominantly Christian. Even chiefs and traditional healers (diviners and herbalists) are nominal if not practising Christians. Nevertheless, the Christianity of the Xhosa is increasingly one which has reached various forms of accommodation with the ancestors and the traditional rituals commemorating them.

Ironically, the ornaments which came to symbolize traditional dress par excellence, particularly in the 20th century, are the product of an indigenous, principally female craft which developed around an introduced item of trade from Europe: the coloured glass bead, which became freely available in the mid-19th century.

SOCIAL ORGANIZATION

Historically, homesteads *(imizi)* tended to be scattered over the rural landscape and were situated on ridges to facilitate drainage and military defence. Dwellings consisted of a circular frame of poles and saplings, which were bent and bound in the shape of a beehive and thatched from top to bottom with grass. To ensure adequate insulation, the inside of the thatch was plastered with a mixture of mud and dung from ground level to about shoulder height. The floor of the dwelling was also plastered with a mixture of mud and dung. A low, rimmed, circular depression in the centre of the floor served as a hearth.

This type of dwelling *(ungquphantsi)* had a low doorway and a person had to stoop to enter it. During the early 1820s this structure was superseded by a more durable and permanent style, which consisted of a circular wattle and daub wall (incorporating methods of construction that had been introduced by missionaries such as Dr. J.T. van der Kemp), supporting a thatched conical roof. The dwellings comprising the homestead were usually grouped in a semi-circle facing onto a large circular brushwood cattle byre, which would have one or more smaller byres situated on its sides for keeping goats. One or more bottle-shaped pits for storing maize were normally located under the floor of the cattle byre. These grain pits were well plastered and sealed with large stones, in order to prevent water seepage and the consequent spoilage of maize through fermentation and rotting. At the best of times, the maize that was stored in these pits had a musty odour and a sour taste, but it was tolerated, and even enjoyed, particularly during the seasons when maize was in short supply.

Also situated outside, behind or adjacent to the houses, were screened-off cooking areas, an earthen oven for baking maize bread *(isonka)* as well as one or more wickerwork bins made of saplings for storing maize on the cob. The swept area between the doorway of the main house and the gateway of the cattle byre was known as the courtyard *(inkundla)*. This was where court cases were heard at the Great Place of a chief or paramount chief. Homesteads were economically self-sufficient entities, with holdings of livestock and lands for cultivation and hunting.

A homestead had a number of houses in which a man, his married sons, their wives and offspring resided. A wealthy man or chief with large cattle herds might have unrelated clients and their families residing at his homestead as well. Such clients provided personal service *(ukubusa)* to the chief or household head, herding his livestock in

BELOW: *Silhouetted against the evening sky, a scarecrow marks the site where the temporary initiation shelter was erected.*

ABOVE: *At the termination of their period of seclusion, the initiates* (abakhwetha), *covered in white blankets, set fire to their makeshift initiation shelter. They must walk away without looking back, thus symbolically turning their backs on their childhood.*

return for the usufruct in milk and progeny, the latter forming the basis of their own herds. Rules of inheritance operated only within the immediate family: the first-born son of the Great Wife inherited his father's livestock. Where polygyny was practised, all the first-born sons of a man's wives stood to inherit a share of his livestock, from which they would build their own herds. Historically land was allocated through the political authorities – i.e. the chief-in-council – and not on the basis of descent groups. Even in cases of wider co-operation between homesteads, for example the ad hoc work parties which are organized to assist in planting, weeding and harvesting, descent is less important than geographical proximity.

The agnatic group (i.e. related through the male line) consists of a cluster of agnatically related household heads and their offspring living in a particular area. Since these men are the descendants of a common great-grandfather, they are very conscious of the group to which they belong. This cluster can vary from 2 or 3 to about 20 household heads. Land and stock is not owned communally by members of the cluster, but is rather held by the individual homesteads within the cluster. These groups have two important, but limited, functions: firstly, to settle disputes between members of the group, and, secondly, to constitute the congregation of the ancestor cult.

Since the patronymic or clan name used by an adult male or female was inherited from his or her father, membership of the agnatic cluster coincided with affiliation to a particular clan. However, the clan was a much wider grouping than the agnatic cluster, which mainly had local importance. The various members of one clan very often lived in different areas and were followers of different clan leaders as well as chiefs. Clan leaders with large followings in a particular chiefdom represented their followers on the chief's council and participated in all decisions affecting the chiefdom. Clan members were descendants of a putative common great-grandfather, although this could not be proved. Members of the same clan did not inter-marry and a woman retained her clan name even after marriage. The clan name still has significance today as an index of social identity. When strangers meet, they very often introduce themselves by mentioning their respective clan names. In this way mutual social connections is identified and established.

The homesteads in a particular area fell under the jurisdiction and authority of the local chief in whose territory they were situated. The Great Place of the chief constituted the social, administrative, judicial and military centre of the chiefdom. Although the executive authority of the chiefdom ultimately rested with the chief's council rather than with the chief himself, the chief was nevertheless the figurehead, the father and bearer of the patronymic of the chiefdom. He convened hunting, harvesting, warfare and circumcision – all co-operative communal activities involving the use of sharp metal instruments such as spears and hoes. These implements were all closely associated with the bush or forest and the shades (spirits), as well as related notions of ritual purity and absention (ukuzila) from meat, sour milk, liquor, tobacco and sexual intercourse. These communal activities therefore involved special sacrificial rites and/or doctoring with medicines. The diviners and herbalists were historically agents of the chief, who made rain in times of drought, doctored the warriors before battle, doctored the cultivated fields to ensure a good harvest, smelt out witches and treated illness and misfortune in man and beast.

The chief's followers were the source of the able-bodied men who served as warriors in the army, defending the chiefdom against rival neighbouring chiefs or foreign incursions. Death dues and fines for murder or witchcraft were payable to the chief in cattle. All the leopard pelts and half the ivory obtained in the hunt accrued to the chief, who was the only person entitled to wear a leopard skin robe (umnweba) and an ivory armband (umxhaka). By 1831 Grahamstown was exporting £50,000 of goods annually, of which £27,000 was made up of hides and £3,000 of ivory purchased from the Xhosa. The Xhosa in return acquired not only regular trade goods (blankets, beads and metal), but also horses and guns.

The followers of the chief contributed cattle towards the bride wealth (lobola) of the chief's Great Wife (see page 24). They attended the annual military review at the Great Place, when the army was doctored by the war-doctor (itola). The ceremony of the first fruits (ulibo) was held at the same time, at which the crops were ritually tasted by the chief before they were harvested in the fields.

As the senior member of a senior lineage, the chief offered sacrifice to the shades on behalf of the chiefdom as a whole. Although Xhosa chiefs belonged to the royal amaTshawe house, this did not necessarily mean that they were politically aligned on all issues all of the time. Political alignments could change depending on the issue at stake. For example, during the epidemic of bovine lung sickness and the Cattle Killing episode which followed it in 1856–7, some Xhosa chiefs supported the Paramount Chief Sarhili's call, which was based on the millennial prophecies of Mhlakaza and Nongqawuse, to destroy all cattle and grain, but others refused to do so. Followers who were disaffected by an unpopular chief could turn their allegiance to a more popular chief. Similarly, an aristocrat, with sufficient political and military support, could usurp the chieftainship from a half-brother or he could move off, colonize new territory and create a new chiefdom of his own. According to Xhosa oral tradition, Tshawe usurped the chieftainship from his half-brother Cirha. As a result of this action, Tshawe, the minor house of Nkosiyamntu, has ever since been the ruling house among the Xhosa. Later, during the 18th century, Chief Phalo's Right-Hand Son Rharhabe crossed the Kei River with his followers after a military clash with his younger half-brother Gcaleka, who was heir to the chieftainship. Rharhabe established his new chiefdom in the Amabele Hills, and the Ciskeian Xhosa came to be known as amaRharhabe, a patronymic which still has relevance today.

The role of the household head, like that of the chief, is an ascribed one determined by birth order and sex and locked into the hierarchy of the descent system. The household head, like the chief, is 'born and not made': he attains his position only after the death of his father. The diviner or herbalist, by contrast, occupies an achieved role. She or he attains office as a healer following a calling, which emanates from the ancestral spirits, and the requisite initiation or training from a practising healer. Thus the healer bypasses the hierarchy of the descent system and can attain office in the lifetime of her or his father.

MARRIAGE

Marriage was traditionally exogamous (marital partners were sought outside the kin group), which was a distinguishing trait of the Nguni in general. Every Nguni child is born into a patrilineal clan and marriage within the clan is a heinous offence and strictly prohibited. Among the Xhosa, who were particularly fastidious in this regard, marriage was avoided with the clans of all four grandparents. Marriage was virilocal, which means that a wife resided with her husband and his people. Marriage was also polygynous, and chiefs and wealthy men with large herds of cattle married more than one wife and, in some instances, had as many as four or more wives. They were usually distinguished in rank according to different houses. Among the Xhosa, the principal cleavage was between the Great House and the Right-Hand House.

Opposite, top: A mother prepares food for the homecoming of the initiates. Opposite, bottom left and right, and pages 22 and 23: Once they have passed menopause, married women are socially on a par with men: they are entitled to smoke a long-stemmed pipe and to attend traditional rituals and beer-drinking occasions.

ABOVE: *Members of a women's-only club dancing at the coming-out of the initiates. Such clubs meet monthly and members contribute money to help each other in times of need.*

The Great Wife was responsible for producing the son and heir, the Great Son, who inherited his father's position – chief or household head as the case may be – after his father's death. The Great Wife of a chief was usually a woman of rank, the daughter of a chief from a neighbouring chiefdom (a Khoisan or Thembu princess). A man's Right-Hand Son, the first-born son of the Right-Hand Wife, was also a chief or household head, with his own herds, dependants and followers. However, he was responsible for establishing his own chiefdom or

homestead by colonizing new or previously unsettled territory. Additional wives were attached as rafters or supports *(amaqadi)* to the two main houses and were distinguished in rank accordingly.

One important consequence of the chief marrying the Great Wife later in life, after contracting other marriages, was that the Great Son and heir was younger than the older and more experienced Right-Hand Son. This was a source of tension and friction between the two half-brothers. The ensuing rivalry between the Right-Hand Son and the Great Son could result in the former usurping the chieftainship of the latter, as in the case of Tshawe and Cirha mentioned earlier. Alternatively, it could lead to fission and segmentation within the chief-dom itself, such as the debacle between Rharhabe and Gcaleka. When a man was monogamous, which was not unusual among commoners, his first wife automatically became the Great Wife and her first-born

son the Great Son and heir. A polygynist's wives each had their own dwellings and economic resources in cattle and grain to maintain their respective households. A chief's Right-Hand Wife usually occupied her own homestead at a distance from the Great Place.

The transfer of cattle *(ikazi)* from the bridegroom's group to the bride's group served both to seal the marriage and compensate the bride's father for the loss of his daughter's labour in his homestead. Marriage negotiations between the two parties could be difficult and protracted, particularly when it came to settling the number of cattle that was to be transferred. The transfer of cattle also served as a form of insurance: should the bride be mistreated in her new home, she could return to her parents' home, and her husband's group would forfeit the cattle. A man who received cattle in exchange for a marriageable daughter could use the cattle to obtain an additional wife for himself or he might use them to assist a son or kinsman to obtain a wife. Thus the exchange of cattle in marriage was a form of circulating bride wealth, with women moving in the opposite direction from the cattle. The missionaries, erroneously believing *lobola* to be the purchase of the bride, condemned the practice on moral grounds.

Although marriages are more commonly contracted in church or the magistrate's court nowadays, *lobola* has not entirely disappeared, even though it is now more likely to be paid in cash equivalent to the market value of the cattle involved in the transaction. Traditional marriage was not simply a means of formalizing a relationship between

THIS PAGE: *Xhosa women with beaded ornaments, dresses, bags and head-dresses. Particularly in the course of the 20th century, such dress has come to be considered as 'traditional' (umbaco) although it is vastly different from the karosses and clothing made from ox hide and animal pelts once worn by the Xhosa.*

members of the opposite sex for the purposes of procreation. More importantly, it was a means of forging alliances between unrelated groups, which is why marriage within the clan was prohibited.

After marriage, the bride effectively a stranger in her new home. She had to show deference and respect *(intlonipho)* to her parents-in-law and all senior members of the homestead; she could not approach the houses directly by walking across the courtyard, but had to approach them from behind; she was also not allowed to enter the cattle byre. A married woman's position within the homestead gradually improved as she had children and they grew up. Menstruating women were considered to be a polluting influence to livestock and were not allowed into the cattle byre. Once they were past menopause, a woman's status was almost on a par with that of men. She was permitted to attend formal beer drinks and sacrifices and to smoke a long-stemmed pipe.

THE ANCESTORS

The effective spirits or shades are typically the deceased senior males of the agnatic group. The Xhosa refer to the ancestors as *iminyanya*, whereas the Mpondo call them the *amathongo*. Notably men of weight and influence during their lives, the shades were leaders of followings – the clan founders, clan leaders and chiefs of the distant past – occupying nodal positions in the kinship structure and with many descendants. The ancestor cult is essentially the cult of the domestic unit, the extended family. As the living link between the members of the homestead and the ancestors of the agnatic group, the male household head officiates on ritual occasions, in person or by proxy.

The deceased household head is incorporated by his sons as an ancestor of the homestead, a process which normally involves two sacrifices. In the first *(umkhapo)*, a white goat without blemish is slaughtered to accompany *(ukukhapa)* the spirit of the deceased to the shades. In the second *(umbuyiso)*, an ox is slaughtered to bring back *(ukubuyisa)* the spirit of the deceased as an ancestor to brood over the eaves and threshold of the homestead. Although historically chiefs were sometimes buried on a river bank or in the forest, household heads were buried in the cattle byre near the gatepost.

All old people who die, women no less than men, become ancestral spirits and can influence the lives of their descendants, communicating with them through dreams and omens. A woman can be an ancestral spirit to her children, her son's children and her brother's children. Although the ancestors of the agnatic group into which she was born continue to influence a woman after marriage, a married woman is nevertheless thought to be influenced by the ancestors of her husband as well. This is articulated symbolically in the traditional wedding ceremony *(umdudo),* when the bride thrusts a spear, belonging to the groom's father, into the gatepost of his cattle byre *(ukuhlalsa umkhonto).*

When a woman is ill or called to become a healer, the head of the homestead where she was born, or his proxy, is obliged to perform the required sacrifice(s) on her behalf.

*THIS PAGE: The bride's entourage and the bride herself (covered in a blanket) taking part in the wedding proceedings. The woman depicted in the bottom right picture is a wedding guest. **PAGE 30, TOP LEFT AND RIGHT:** The bride's party (uduli) arriving at the home of the groom's family for the traditional wedding ceremony (umdudo). **PAGE 30, BOTTOM:** The bridegroom (third from left) with a group of well-wishers, including Winnie Madikizela-Mandela (second from left). **PAGE 31:** The wedding of Nkosi Patekile Sango Holomisa and Princess Bukelwa Matanzima. In the case of a royal wedding such as this one, the act of ukuhlalsa umkhonto (see main text, this page) endows the new bride with the status of ndlunkulu (senior wife) which entitles her to bear the royal heir. The senior wife is not permitted to remarry after the death of her husband.*

BELOW, LEFT AND RIGHT: Men indulging in drinking and smoking. At the initiates' coming-out ceremony (umgidi) older men offer a harangue, during which the young men are exhorted to be men, to care for their parents and maintain the household. BOTTOM: Villagers mark their sheep as a deterrent to stock theft. OPPOSITE: Elderly women at their traditional home (isithembiso), in the rural area near East London.

Quite apart from illness and misfortune, traditional rituals *(amasiko)* are performed at virtually every stage of the life-cycle, from birth through puberty, marriage and menopause to death. The Cape Nguni utilize a whole repertoire of metaphors in reference to the spirits and the spiritual world. Probably one of the oldest of these metaphors used for the ancestors is wind *(umoya)*, a term which was adopted by the

missionaries for the Holy Spirit and has been used in Xhosa translations of the Bible ever since. Traditional rituals are still widely performed today, although in considerably altered and attenuated form, both in the rural areas and in the suburbs of South African towns and cities.

RITES OF PASSAGE

Some 150 years ago or more, all southern African chiefdoms and Khoisan peoples observed initiation practices to prepare the youth, male and female, for their future roles in adult society. At some unknown date in the past, the Xhosa chiefdom adopted circumcision as the principal form of male initiation, possibly from a Sotho source, and it has become closely associated with them ever since. In the course of time and largely as a result of Xhosa influence, circumcision was adopted by neighbouring chiefdoms such as the Thembu, Mfengu, Bomvana,

Xesibe, Mpondo and Mpondomise. Undoubtedly, circumcision originally had a militaristic significance, as a worthy ordeal for the young men who were to serve as warriors before being eligible to marry. When Dingiswayo, Shaka's predecessor, introduced the regimental system in Zululand (see page 34), Zulu circumcision was discontinued.

In the past, every Xhosa initiate was presented with spears and war clubs by his father and father's brothers at the coming-out ceremony (umgidi) held to incorporate the initiates (abakhwetha) back into society from the bush where they had been secluded. Circumcision continues to be practised in attenuated form by Xhosa-speakers, both in towns and rural areas, although its efficacy is presently questionable from a medical point of view. Since the early 1990s, the numbers of male initiates who suffer medical and psychiatric complications, and even die, as a result of the circumcision operation has been increasing every year. The solution to these vexing problems obviously lies in placing the circumcision operation itself in the hands of medically trained personnel.

THE ZULU

The origin of the Zulu, probably the largest single population group in South Africa,

lies in a small Nguni-speaking chiefdom that emerged near the White Umfolozi River

in what is today known as KwaZulu-Natal during the 16th century. Shaka, who

became the chief of the tiny Zulu group in 1818, laid the foundations of the Zulu

nation and built the mightiest empire in southern Africa.

Around 1550 Malandela, a chief with a small following, settled at the foot of Amandawe Hill on the southern banks of the Umhlatuze River just before it enters the Nkwaleni Valley. He had two sons, Qwabe and Zulu, who, according to oral tradition, constantly squabbled with one another, and so Malandela sent Qwabe to live along the lower reaches of the river, somewhere near present-day Empangeni, and Zulu was sent north to settle in the region of the White Umfolozi River. In due course, both brothers consolidated their followings into separate clans, and both paid separate tribute *(ukukhonza)* to the Mthethwa chief, who was the most powerful in the region.

Towards the end of the 18th century Dingiswayo became the chief of the Mthethwa. As a young man, he had had to flee for his life, as his father suspected he was plotting to overthrow him. Dingiswayo travelled extensively throughout the region that is today known as KwaZulu-Natal. Through his travels, his vision was broadened and he was introduced to trading, which was growing steadily around the Portuguese port of Delagoa Bay. When he heard about the death of his father, he returned on horseback, carrying a gun, to take over the leadership of the Mthethwa.

Dingiswayo was a shrewd and powerful leader who recognized that competition for land and natural resources was becoming more and more intense and that ability to dominate trade with the Portuguese would bring distinct advantages. Thus he saw that building up the Mthethwa army and his following was increasingly important. To this end, he set about systematically amalgamating into a single polity the loosely structured groups that paid tribute to him, and absorbing those whom he defeated in combat.

Around 1787, Senzangakhona, the young chief of the Zulu (which derived its name from one of Malandela's quarrelsome sons), fathered a son out of wedlock, Shaka. After serving a number of years in Dingiswayo's army, where he excelled as a military tactician and officer, Shaka became the Zulu chief on his father's death. At that time the

Zulu were a small group of possibly 1,500 people, which Shaka was determined to build into the major role-player in the political development of the subcontinent. From the handful of men he could muster among the Zulu, he created an embryo army which, over a period of 12 years, he formed into a formidable fighting force that eventually included the armies of formerly independent neighbouring groups. In doing so, he transformed his small chiefdom into the mighty Zulu nation.

In 1828 Shaka was assassinated by his half-brothers, Dingane and Mhlangana. After bitter squabbling between the two brothers and their supporters, Dingane gained the upper hand and took over the leadership of the Zulu empire. Dingane lacked the military genius of Shaka and the leadership qualities required to hold his empire together, and so the edifice that Shaka had created began to crumble. Rebel chiefs broke away and Dingane did not have the ability to force them back.

White settlers were beginning to arrive in colonial Natal in increasing numbers, adding new tensions to those turbulent times. The green hills were seen by the Voortrekkers (disgruntled white farmers who had emigrated from the eastern Cape) as their new eldorado, and they made overtures to Dingane for land on which they could settle and establish their farms. The Zulu king feared that this would be the thin end of a wedge which would eventually topple him from his throne, and so he had Piet Retief, the Voortrekker emissary who had come to negotiate with him, and his companions put to death. He also sent his

TOP: In the past, geometric designs were often carved into earplugs, but these are now generally decorated with brightly coloured pieces of plastic. OPPOSITE: Young women from the Nongoma area at the Reed Ceremony, which was first introduced in 1984. Beadwork from the Nongoma area includes the use of square or rectangular blocks of green, red, black and sometimes yellow beads.

The defeat was humiliating and the backbone of Dingane's power was irreparably cracked. However, his army was only finally defeated when Mpande, Dingane's remaining half-brother, who had amassed a considerable following and built a powerful army, attacked him on the Maqongqo hills near the Swaziland border. Dingane, now a refugee Zulu king with a handful of followers, tried to flee to Swaziland but was killed before he reached there. Mpande, the longest reigning monarch in Zulu history, succeeded Dingane to the throne and ruled over a much

LEFT: Young women attending the Reed Ceremony, which is held at King Goodwill Zwelethini's Enkoyeni Palace in the Nongoma area, travel from as far afield as Ixopo in southern KwaZulu-Natal in buses rented for the occasion. BELOW: Some of the beadwork styles worn by young women attending the Reed Ceremony include words or slogans. This practice is especially common among communities living in the Msinga area south of the Thukela River, and on the south coast of KwaZulu-Natal. OPPOSITE: Married women escort the girls who travel to King Zwelethini's royal residence to attend the Reed Ceremony. These women sometimes join in the dancing, but their impromptu appearances are generally short-lived.

army to kill their women and children and the men guarding the Voortrekker camps at distant Bloukrans, near present-day Estcourt. Those who survived swore, in a covenant with God, to avenge their deaths and to build a church in His honour if victory in battle against the Zulu were granted to them. On 16 December 1838 on the banks of the Ncome River, which was renamed Blood River, revenge was ruthlessly and bloodily exacted. Over 3,000 Zulu warriors were killed in battle, while only the Voortrekker leader sustained a minor injury.

reduced Zulu kingdom from 1840 to his death in 1872. Mpande had been considered harmless, if not an idiot, by Dingane, and so had been spared when Dingane rid himself of all perceived sibling threats on accession to the throne. However, he proved to be a shrewd ruler who played both ends of the political spectrum – maintaining a dignified but qualified subservience to his white neighbours in the Colony of Natal south of the Thukela River, while retaining control over and the loyalty of his followers north of the river.

After his death, his son, Cetshwayo, became the new king in 1872. He was a forceful man who steadily reinstated much of the military discipline his uncle, Shaka, had developed some 50 years before; with this came a resurgence of Zulu pride and sense of destiny. The spectre of a militant Zulu nation north of the Thukela began to send tremors through the fabric of colonial Natal. Queen Victoria's officers were determined to see English control extended across Africa, from the Cape to Cairo. Zulu power was viewed as a major threat to this vision, and war between England and the Zulu became inevitable. It began after an impossible ultimatum issued by the British to the Zulu was ignored. The first major clash was at Isandlwana on 21 January 1879 when the Zulu inflicted the largest defeat the British army suffered in

its colonial history. The war ended at Ulundi on 4 July of the same year, when Cetshwayo's military headquarters at Ondini were razed to the ground and his armies routed.

The Colonial Office took over the administration of Zululand and immediately set about reducing the power of the royal house by dividing political power between 13 independent chieftainships. This led to a smouldering civil war, a period of continued strife and the increasing intervention of the Natal colonial administration in the government and control of Zulu affairs. With the advent of Union in 1910 and white control over the whole of South Africa, white absolute power was entrenched and the Zulu king's hope of attaining state recognition became increasingly remote. The status of Cetshwayo's son, Dinuzulu, and his grandson, Solomon, was reduced to that of an ordinary chief, charged with little more than control over a small area of what had once been the Zulu kingdom. It was only in the 1950s that the Nationalist government appointed King Cetshwayo's great-grandson, Cyprian, as paramount of the Zulu. However, the present king's powers are essentially symbolic. As such, he carries a sacred axe *(inhlendla)* on important state occasions, and he presides over key rituals, among them the annual Reed Ceremony, which was first introduced in 1984.

ABOVE: *Regional variations in the styles of the clothing and beadwork worn at the Reed Ceremony by both married women and unmarried girls attest to the diverse histories and traditions of Zulu-speaking traditionalists. The woman who is at the centre of this group is from the Ixopo district.* **OPPOSITE, TOP:** *The girls who attend the Reed Ceremony are led by the king's daughters and other princesses.* **OPPOSITE, BOTTOM LEFT AND RIGHT:** *The reeds are gathered to build a new dwelling, which is said to symbolize the willingness of the girls to work together. Once these girls have passed in front of the king, they lay the reeds down at the new building site.*

SOCIAL ORGANIZATION

Kin forms the basis of Zulu traditional life, which is centred on the *umuzi* (extended homestead). Until quite recently, the *umuzi* consisted of the headman *(umnumzane)*, with his wives and children, his younger brothers with their wives and families, and, in many cases, married sons as well. With urbanization and the break-up of past social structures, the *umuzi* has become smaller and smaller, often including only one man and his wife (or wives) and children. Traditionally, the extended homestead was a self-contained economic unit, in which a complete

life could be led. Each *umuzi* had its own cattle and supply of milk, and its own fields on which maize and vegetables were grown to supply the needs of the inhabitants of the extended homestead.

The architecture and layout of the *umuzi* were the same throughout Zulu society and reflected the status of the different wives. The positions of the wives of a commoner were regulated according to the order in which they were married, the first wife being the chief wife *(inkosikazi)*. With the king and important chiefs, the great wife, who was rarely the first wife, was chosen in consultation with the king's advisers after he had reached adulthood and was eligible to wear the *isicoco* (head-ring) *(see page 50).*

The chief wife occupied the chief dwelling *(indlunkulu)*, at the top of the *umuzi*, directly opposite the main entrance. Her eldest son was, and in traditional society still is, the chief heir and successor to his father, and he also occupied an important position in religious matters. On the right of the main entrance of the *umuzi*, next to the chief dwelling, was the right-hand wife *(iqadi)*, who fulfilled a supplementary role to the chief wife. One of her functions was to provide an heir should the chief wife fail to bear a son. On the left was the left-hand wife *(ikhohlo)* who occupied the second position of dignity in the *umuzi*. In the case of a chief, the left-hand wife was often the first wife he married. She, with all the subordinate wives who formed part of her household *(amabibi)*, were entirely independent of the chief dwelling.

The *umuzi* was roughly circular in form and was built on sloping ground facing east wherever possible, with the slope falling away to the main entrance, so that the chief dwelling would be on the highest ground and would overlook the rest of the *umuzi*. In the centre was the cattle byre *(isibaya)* where the cattle were corralled at night and the grain was stored in underground pits. The perimeter of the byre is normally built out of closely packed stakes or, if there are no trees in the vicinity, out of stones. The cattle byre could be likened to the *umuzi's* temple: it was, and in many rural areas still is, the place where the ancestral spirits are thought to linger and thus where prayers are held. Here sacrifices are made and thanks offered for blessings received (*see* page 62). In the past, women generally did not enter the cattle byre, and no woman who was not a 'child of the house' was allowed entry,

except on special occasions. However, during the 20th century, the tendency among men to seek work as migrants has forced many women to take responsibility for their husbands' livestock.

Traditionally individual dwellings were built between the fence of the cattle byre and the outer fence *(uthango)* of the *umuzi*, around which prickly pear or acacia trees with long thorns were planted to provide a

LEFT: *Young women first wear the leather skirts* (isidwaba) *that are associated with married women at their coming-of-age* (umemulo) *ceremonies. In some areas, the beadwork garments worn over these skirts are now made from large plastic beads. This means that the beaded garments are not only much cheaper than those made from glass beads, but also much quicker to execute.* **BELOW:** *The* umemulo *ceremony is held to mark the transition from girlhood to womanhood. The ceremonies are usually held once the girl has met her future husband and is about to marry, but ceremonies of this kind may also be held to indicate that the girl is ready to receive potential suitors.* **OPPOSITE, TOP:** *Women preparing food for a girl's* umemulo *ceremony. An ox is slaughtered for the guests, and the caul of fat* (umhlwehlwe) *surrounding its stomach is worn by the girl for part of the ceremony.* **OPPOSITE, BOTTOM:** *Married women at an* umemulo *ceremony. Even though many married women no longer wear leather skirts, they still cover their shoulders with shawls, or tie a scarf diagonally across their torsos, as a sign of respect to the ancestors* (amabhayi).

*OPPOSITE: Young women demonstrating their dancing skills at an umemulo ceremony; one of them is wearing the checked towel that is commonly used by young Zulu-speaking traditionalists from the area north of the Thukela River. The adoption of ski pants for these demonstrations is comparatively new, but the use of ankle rattles made from the seed pods of indigenous plants has probably been in use for several centuries. **ABOVE:** A young man pins money to a young woman's head-dress. The money that is donated by guests and relatives at a coming-of-age ceremony is used to buy her dowry. **TOP RIGHT:** A procession led by the father of a young woman at her coming-of-age ceremony includes 'bridesmaids' who also wear the leather skirts associated with married women, and, in some cases, younger, pre-pubescent girls. **RIGHT:** In most cases, the caul of fat worn by young women at their coming-of-age ceremonies is cooked and eaten, together with the meat from the ox which has been slaughtered for this occasion.*

measure of protection against invaders. Building, which was considered to be men's work, was done communally in the form of a social event *(ilima)*. A man would instruct his wives to brew beer and inform his neighbours of his intention to build a dwelling. On the appointed day, many people would turn up and even passers-by were expected to lend a hand. Traditional Zulu dwellings were either beehive- or dome-shaped and made by embedding a row of pointed saplings as deeply as possible in a circular trench dug some 15 centimetres (6 inches) deep and 5 metres (16 feet) in diameter. The saplings were bent over and tied down to create a circular framework, which was then tightly thatched. There were no windows and the doorway was so low that people had to enter on hands and knees. At night it was closed by means of a wicker door fastened with a cross-stick. The floor was made of a mixture of ant-heap and clay, which was beaten hard with stones, plastered with cow-dung *(ubulongo)* and smoothed over with flat stones. Once dry, it was rubbed until it was hard and highly polished *(ukugudula)*. Traditionally the right side of these dwellings was for men and the left for women. Cooking was done inside in a demarcated hearth *(iziko)* about 1½ metres (5 feet) from the door. No attempt was made to evacuate the smoke through a chimney; it was allowed to rise and seep randomly through the walls and roof.

LIFE IN THE EXTENDED HOMESTEAD

A traditional Zulu *umuzi* was well regulated by strict etiquette and social discipline. Although a man might have a number of wives, there were seldom clashes or jealousy, as the wives were all independent. Each had her own home, and fields and cattle were appointed to her for her use. All members of the *umuzi* had their place and function, but their status changed as they grew older. A bride, at first under the control of her mother-in-law, became a mother herself, and then a grand-mother, and finally a respected elder in the community. A boy first

Top left and right, and above: *Celebrations at a wedding of the* Ibandla lamaNazaretha *(the 'Shembe church'). Most members of this independent church are staunch traditionalists who pay homage to the ancestors and praise God through songs and dances punctuated by the sound of whistles, bugles and drums.* ***Bottom right:*** *The bride and groom, Zanele Mthembu and Patrick Zithulele.* ***Opposite, top:*** *Married women of the* Ibandla lamaNazaretha *wearing beadwork garments made in the distinctive styles of this group.* ***Opposite, bottom:*** *The women of this church always carry umbrellas and little dance shields.*

herded goats and then cattle. After this he graduated to the status of a young man with special responsibilities and, until the destruction of the Zulu kingdom in 1879, military duties. After fulfilling these duties for some years, he was allowed to become a husband and father; in due course he was accepted as an adult member of the council of elders. Every individual passed through a number of well-marked stages, none of which could be entered into without preparation and ceremony (see page 47).

Childbirth among the Zulu has always been the concern of women alone, and no men are allowed to be present at birth. Midwives are older women of the *umuzi* who are past child-bearing age. After babies are born, they are washed in the *umsamo* (a sacred section at the back of the dwelling) with water medicated with *intelezi* (special medicine), and then they are 'strengthened' by the observance of rituals and the application of strengthening medicines. Even today, both mothers and children are then isolated, usually until the umbilical cord falls off. During this time the mothers are considered 'unclean' and potentially harmful to the ancestors in their husbands' homesteads. They are not allowed to touch ordinary utensils and have to eat food prepared by the midwives, out of a special dish, using a special spoon.

The isolation normally lasts five to ten days, after which the mother is purified: she has to be sprinkled with *intelezi* before she can resume her normal life. The dwelling has to be thoroughly cleaned, fresh cow-dung spread on the floor and a fire lit in the hearth. After this, the husband may enter and see his child for the first time, although today migrant fathers are seldom able to come home for these events. Beer is brewed to celebrate and to thank the midwives. This occasion is repeated when the father comes home from the city to meet his child.

In the past, daily life in an *umuzi* followed roughly the same routine. A clear distinction was made on the basis of sex, age and rank. The young boys were responsible for taking the cattle out into the veld to graze; the girls, either on their own or with their mothers, went to the river to fetch water. Thus Zulu children were exposed to nature at an early age, inculcating a deep, lasting understanding and empathy for the environment in which they lived. After breakfast, usually served mid-morning, the women busied themselves sweeping, cleaning pots and doing other domestic chores. In summer, early in the day while it was still cool, they would go to the fields to weed their crops.

OPPOSITE, TOP LEFT: Bride and groom, Zanele Mthembu and Patrick Zithulele of the Ibandla lamaNazaretha. The money pinned to the bride's head-dress is donated by well-wishers. OPPOSITE, TOP RIGHT: On certain occasions, members of the Ibandla lamaNazaretha wear long white robes. In addition to these robes, most have large wardrobes including leather garments, beadwork items, hats and head-dresses. OPPOSITE, BOTTOM: The bride dancing at her wedding. Brides sometimes wear aprons made from the skins of wild animals. These are similar to the 'pregnancy aprons' married women adopt after conception and may indicate either that the bride is already pregnant or her unequivocal desire to conceive a child. ABOVE: A married member of the Ibandla lamaNazaretha dancing at a wedding. The style of the beadwork panel attached to her head-dress includes the use of metallic colours which has become increasingly common among members of this church since the mid-1980s. TOP RIGHT: During some parts of the ceremony, the bride wears a veil as a sign of respect to her future in-laws and their ancestors. PAGE 48: Shaka Day celebrations were first introduced in the 1970s, when KwaZulu became an independent governing territory under the apartheid state. These celebrations are held on the anniversary of the death of the first Zulu king, who was assassinated in September 1828.

In the late morning the herdboys would return with the cattle, which were milked in the cattle byre. After milking, the first meal of the day was eaten. Cooking was done on a hearth within the dwelling in a large cooking pot *(ikhanzi)*. Then, as now, *amasi* (curds of milk) formed an important part of the diet: it was eaten either on its own or mixed with maize meal or vegetables. To this day, another staple, maize meal, is produced in some homesteads by laboriously grinding corn between two rocks. This meal is either boiled into a thick porridge *(uphutu)*, or added to *amasi* or an assortment of vegetables. Before the advent of stores with refrigeration facilities, meat was eaten only on special occasions, such as at a wedding, or when a sacrifice was made to celebrate an important event, for instance welcoming an honoured guest.

After breakfast the boys would take the cattle back to pasture and the women returned to their household duties. As the day began to cool, the women either shouldered their hoes and returned to their fields to continue hoeing, planting and weeding, or they went out to fetch firewood. Men were less involved in domestic chores and spent much of their time attending meetings in the *ibandla* (chief's court), a recognized meeting place usually under trees outside the *umuzi*, or doing private work, such as repairing their shields or working skins.

Women were, and still are, responsible for mat-making and beadwork, which they learn from their mothers. Pottery is a highly skilled craft practised by comparatively few. All woodwork is done by men, who usually specialize in making particular items, like spoons, meat trays and milk pails, which are carved from solid pieces of wood. Hardly any carvers still make headrests because people now prefer to use pillows. Blacksmithing was a specialized profession, traditionally practised in secret and often restricted to the male members of one family only. The main items made were hoes, for cultivating the fields, and the blades of spears, the principal weapons of war. From about the 1830s, the major source of metal was through trade with the English and Portuguese. Beads, cloth, brass and muskets were exchanged for ivory, labour, skins and cattle. This trade resulted in the rapid demise of traditional iron-smelting skills, as more easily smithed, but inferior, raw iron became increasingly accessible from passing traders.

INDIVIDUAL DEVELOPMENT

In the past Zulu traditional life was highly structured and discipline underlined its every facet. Each person had a place and specific functions to perform, depending on gender, and age and rank in the *umuzi*. Distinction between members of the *umuzi* was reinforced by the fact that every individual passed through a number of well-marked stages, none of which could be entered into without preparation and ceremony. The first stage in the transition from childhood to adulthood was marked by the *qhumbuza* or ear-piercing ceremony, which every child had to undergo before reaching puberty.

The next stage in the life of the individual was the attainment of physical maturity, or puberty. In early times, this was the occasion for an important initiation ceremony called the *thomba*, which applied equally to boys and girls. During the initiation process, boys and girls of the same age went into separate seclusion, where they were taught by instructors on the requirements and duties of adulthood. The period of seclusion was done away with after the introduction of the *amabutho* (age-based regiments) system in the late 18th century. After the male *thomba* ceremony, the young boy was called an *insizwa* (young man) and he was free to court girls of his age and in his group, but he was not free to marry. Two further rites of passage had to be performed before this was possible. The first was his incorporation into a regiment, or *ibutho*, which could involve as many as 10 years of service to the king. The second was the sewing on of the *isicoco* or head-ring, which signified the attainment of full adulthood.

After the destruction of the Zulu kingdom, the formation of age-grade regiments was banned, and the traditions associated with them eventually disappeared. However, recently, the Zulu royal family has

PAGE 49, TOP: Prince Gideon Zulu at Shaka Day celebrations. PAGE 49, BOTTOM: Prince Gideon Zulu, Chief Mangosuthu Buthelezi and King Goodwill Zwelethini lead Shaka Day proceedings. The crane feathers of the prince and king signal their royal status; the sacred axe carried by the king affirms his role as mediator between the Zulu and the royal family's ancestors. TOP LEFT: Gifts presented at a wedding by the bride's family usually include a kist, grass mats and blankets. TOP RIGHT: Stick-fighting (ukuncweka) at a wedding. Displays of this martial art are common at weddings as it serves to underline a man's virility. ABOVE LEFT AND RIGHT: Graduation ceremony of a diviner (isangoma). The money pinned to her head-dress is consistent with the pinning of money to head-dresses at coming-of-age ceremonies and weddings; her knife is used in the slaughter of animals and in digging up ingredients for preparing medicines. OPPOSITE: Graduation ceremonies of diviners and healers usually include ritual slaughtering of a goat and an ox, which are traditionally stabbed to death. Diviners may paint their faces white to acknowledge their association with the shades from the underworld, who are said to be white.

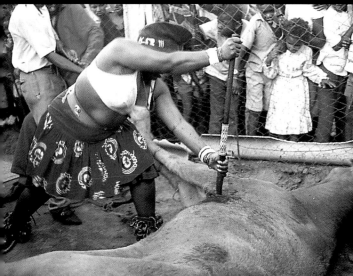
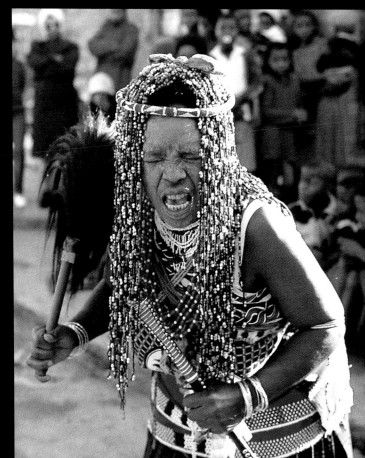

sought to revive past practices and has introduced a number of new ones, like Shaka Day celebrations and the Reed Ceremony. The Reed Ceremony, which aims to inculcate a sense of pride in young women, has become a major event, attended by girls from the entire KwaZulu-Natal region. Since 1994, when the African National Congress came to power, attempts have been made to transform this ceremony into a multi-cultural event, but these have not been entirely successful.

PAGES 52 AND 53: Diviners usually wear long white, beaded head-dresses in acknowledgement of their association with the shades of the underworld. Most diviners are female but men may also enter this profession if called by the ancestors to do so. Many of these male diviners cross-dress and may also learn to fashion the beaded items commonly worn by diviners. BELOW: Dr. Sibongile Zungu, now the medical superintendent at the Catherine Booth Hospital near Amatikulu, made history when she was appointed chief following the untimely death of her husband in the early 1990s. The beadwork items worn by her and her two daughters were given to them by members of the Ibandla lamaNazaretha, *many of whom live in the ward formerly under her husband's jurisdiction.*

Young women also have coming-of-age ceremonies *(umemulo)*. At these, the woman's family slaughters an ox from which she obtains a caul of fat which she wears while dancing for the assembled guests. This fat symbolizes the protection her ancestors will afford her when she leaves her home to marry and live in another homestead.

MILITARY ORGANIZATION

During the reign of Shaka and his successors, the growth and strength of the Zulu nation lay in its military organization and skills. The military was organized around the system of *ukubuthwa* (to be enrolled) which largely did away with initiation ceremonies. In terms of the system, each age-set, that is a group of young men of the same age, was incorporated into the same regiment *(ibutho* singular, *amabutho* plural). *Ukubuthwa* also applied to girls, but in most cases they belonged to an age-set rather than a regiment. The *amabutho* were accommodated at military barracks *(ikhanda* singular, *amakhanda* plural) throughout the kingdom, which were under the control of a close relative of the king or someone appointed by him. The barracks were similar in design and layout to the ordinary *umuzi*, but on a much larger scale. In addition to military duties, the *izinsizwa* (young men) were involved in the repair

THIS PAGE: Married women who observe tradition wear leather skirts, and beaded grass belts and aprons. Beaded aprons date to the mid-19th century, when beads became freely available. In recent years, women have begun to use small bottles, safety pins and plastic items on their leather skirts and other garments. *PAGE 56:* Head-dress styles vary widely depending on marital status. The designs on the head-dress of the married woman at the top identify her as a member of the Ibandla lamaNazaretha. The women at the bottom have begun to grow their hair for their weddings, when they adopt the large head-dresses of married women. In the past, these were built up from the woman's hair, which was covered in clay and red ochre; today detachable head-dresses are more common.

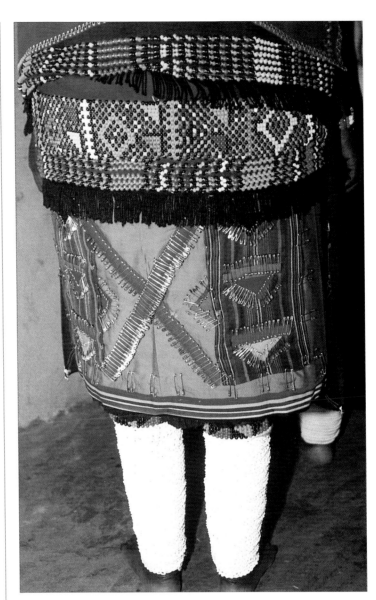

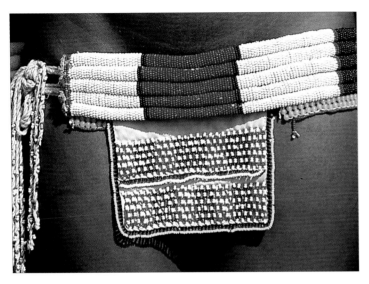

PAGE 57: *A married woman of the Ibandla lamaNazaretha. In the past she would have worn large round earplugs in her stretched earlobes, but this practice is becoming increasingly uncommon.* **ABOVE AND LEFT:** *Most married women from the Thukela Ferry area wear wide, disk-like head-dresses. Some of these women also have earrings that emulate the once common practice among male and female traditionalists of wearing earplugs.* **OPPOSITE, TOP:** *A married woman's head-dress from the Valley of a Thousand Hills, between Pietermaritzburg and Durban.* **OPPOSITE, BOTTOM LEFT:** *A woman who has begun to grow her hair in preparation for her wedding.* **OPPOSITE, BOTTOM RIGHT:** *An older married woman with stretched earlobes. In the past, all Zulu-speakers stretched their earlobes in this way, not only for aesthetic, but also for religious reasons.*

and maintenance of their barracks and were called upon to perform duties at both their barracks and the royal residence. They functioned as keepers of the national herd, messengers for the king and domestic policemen, and also saw to crop production for the royal household. An important feature of military organization was that there were always men undergoing a period of military training and so it was easy for the king to assemble an effective military force at short notice.

Fighting techniques devised by Shaka were revolutionary and played a significant role in the rise of Zulu military and political power. The first thing Shaka did was to change traditional fighting tactics. Prior to his reign, opposing armies had lined up and lobbed their spears at each other. Shaka introduced close hand-to-hand combat using long-bladed, short-shafted stabbing spears. He reduced shields to more manageable proportions and trained his men to use their shields to hook their opponent's shield and wrench it aside, thus exposing his left flank to the Zulu warrior's spear. Shaka also developed a strategy of concentrating his soldiers into a fighting formation resembling a buffalo head. In the centre or 'chest' was the greatest concentration of men, comprising the most experienced fighters. They were deployed in two parallel formations, so that the soldiers in the front would engage the enemy, while those in the rear would be hidden from sight. This strategy was designed firstly to deceive the enemy into believing that they were being opposed by a relatively small force, and secondly so that the soldiers held in reserve would be able to reinforce the frontline soldiers if necessary. As they would be fresh, they could also chase and outdistance the defeated enemy in retreat. Emanating from the chest were two horns whose purpose was to encircle the enemy. When attacking, a common tactic was to feint with one horn, while the other, concealed in the bush and long grass could sweep around unseen to surround the enemy. These tactics proved to be a decisive factor in the Zulu kingdom's dramatic rise to power.

When a regiment had accomplished a certain period of service to the king, which could be up to 10 years, the king would decree that the members of a particular age-set could marry and sew on the head-ring. One of the results of controlling the age at which men could marry was a balance in Zulu society between population growth and available resources.

POLITICAL ORGANIZATION

The political organization of the Zulu was built like a pyramid. At the base of the structure were the individual households *(imizi)*, which comprised the smallest political units in the government of the nation. Each *umuzi* was under the control of the *umnumzane* (household head) *(see page 38)*, who was responsible for keeping order and dealing with any domestic or local disputes that might arise. He was responsible to the *induna* – the head of the district *(isigodi)* in which the *umuzi* was situated. The head of the district was responsible for all law and order in his district and settled disputes which the household head could not settle or which were too large or important for him to handle. The district in turn formed part of a larger region, the *isifunda*, which was controlled by an important district head or hereditary chief

OPPOSITE, TOP: *The comparatively recent practice of wearing bifurcated horn-like head-dresses is restricted to married women who trace their ancestry to the Thukela Ferry area.* ***OPPOSITE, BOTTOM:*** *A young woman preparing for her wedding often wears a black hairnet.* ***ABOVE:*** *Brewing sorghum beer is still common among rural traditionalists. The beer is usually served three days after it has cooled.*

(inkosi), who was directly responsible to the king. In a land and at a time when communications were physically difficult to achieve, this interlocking pyramidal political structure provided an effective way for the king to exercise political control over his kingdom.

Much of this structure has survived the interference of successive white administrations, and South Africa's new democratic government, elected in 1994, has acknowledged the need to support and maintain traditional structures of authority in the interest of rural stability. However, some traditional practices are in conflict with the provisions contained in South Africa's new constitution, which guarantees equality regardless of race, religious affiliation or gender. The allocation of land to women, which would not have been allowed in the past, has therefore become increasingly common.

MEDICINE AND MAGIC

Traditional medicines in Zulu society have their origins in the mists of antiquity; and their use and application today have changed little over the ages. The Zulu make a distinction between the herbalist *(inyanga yokwelapha)*, whose task it is, still today, to administer medicines made from plants and animals, and the diviner *(inyanga yokubhula)*, who 'smells out' or divines the cause of complaints by using bones, shells, seeds and other artefacts. The diviner keeps these items in a special container which he or she throws on a mat, much like the throwing of dice, and from the way they land is able to divine the client's problems. There are two other categories of diviners: the *isangoma* is a medium who can make contact with the ancestral spirits and prescribe medicines according to their dictates, which are then obtained from the *inyanga yokubhula*; the *isanusi* is a diviner capable of 'smelling out' sorcerers and other evil-doers.

The *inyanga* (plural *izinyanga*) and *isangoma* acquire their knowledge and skills over a long apprenticeship which in traditional society could span as long as 20 years. Traditionally medicine men and women occupied a very high status in the community, often second only to the chief. In modern urban society this status has largely been translated into wealth. Most *izinyanga* in urban areas have shops in which they have consulting rooms and from which they dispense and sell their medicines.

MUSIC

Music, song and dancing have traditionally played an important part in Zulu life, not only of the individual, but also of the community as a whole. Dance has always been important in maintaining a sense of group solidarity, particularly during times of stress, joy and change, for example, before battles, at weddings and at all the important transition ceremonies marking entry to a new stage or group (usually an age-set).

Musical instruments were not used in most traditional Zulu dances, and neither was the drum, so common in other groups. Indeed, the only drum known in early traditional Zulu culture was the *iNgungu*, or pot-drum, which was made by stretching a piece of goat-skin over the mouth of a large earthen pot *(imbiza)* and played by tapping with the hand. From available records, it would appear that the *isigubu*, or wooden drum, that is common among the Zulu today was copied, possibly from their Thonga neighbours. The Zulu had a number of stringed instruments of which the *uGubu*, a stringed bow with a calabash attached at one end, was the best known.

Dancing has always had great ritual value in the lives of the Zulu, and there are many occasions in Zulu life when it forms a vital part of the ceremonial procedure for important events. For example, when a boy or girl reaches puberty, specific songs are sung, accompanied by much dancing. The same applies to marriage, where the ritualized mutual antagonism between the two parties is portrayed by an elaborate dancing competition that forms an important part of every wedding ceremony. Especially in the past, when hunting was still common, dancing also had ritual value before a hunt. Prior to setting out, the men gathered in the cattle byre where they danced, boasting of their prowess and what they would do and how brave they would be on the hunt. In this way, enthusiasm for the hunt was stimulated and expectations heightened. The most spectacular and imposing of all Zulu dancing was that of the king's regiments in full regimental dress prior to battle and at the annual dances at the king's palace just after the Feast of the First Fruits. The soldiers' dancing routines were energetic and powerful, precise in timing and posture and very well rehearsed. The effect of this, combined with their elaborate regimental attire, was awesome indeed.

RELIGION AND BELIEFS

Throughout Zulu history, there has been hardly an aspect of traditional Zulu life in which religion has not played a part: in warfare, in ceremonies, in the different stages and crises in people's personal lives, in agriculture and economic well-being and so on. At all times, the ancestors are looked upon as the source from which help and guidance can be derived after appropriate propitiation through sacrificial offerings. In addition to the respect they show their ancestors, the Zulu also believed in a supernatural being, *Unkulunkulu*, who 'sprang from a bed of reeds' and who created all wild animals, cattle and game, snakes and birds, water and mountains, as well as the sun and the moon.

According to Zulu beliefs, human beings have a body *(umzimba)* and a spirit or soul *(idlozi)*. In addition, there is the *inhliziyo* (heart or feelings), the *ingqondo* (brain, mind, understanding) and the *isithunzi* (shadow, personality). The Zulu believe that the *isithunzi* becomes the ancestral spirit after death, but only after the *ukubuyisa* ceremony has been performed, during which the spirit is 'brought back home'.

Sacrifice plays an important role in maintaining contact with the ancestral spirits, providing a 'bridge' which enables the individual to ask for favours or to thank the ancestral spirits for their blessings. Ancestral spirits are believed to have the power to regulate the forces of nature and are approached before all important events.

The Zulu distinguish two classes of sacrifice. The thanksgiving *(ukubonga)* takes place when something good has come about, such as when a boy reaches puberty, when there is plenty of food, or when life in the *umuzi* has gone smoothly and there has been little sickness. The *ukuthetha*, a scolding sacrifice, takes place when people of the *umuzi* die unexpectedly, or when things seem to go wrong and the individual feels persecuted. All sacrifices, which are usually of cattle or goats, are performed according to ritual and the strict observation of procedure and protocol, since, if these are not followed, the sacrifice may not only bring about no benefits, but could even be detrimental.

During the 20th century, many traditionalists have become members of one of the independent churches, which seek to combine Christian practice with respect for the ancestors. One of these, the *Ibandla lamaNazaretha*, is especially popular among rural Zulu. Founded in 1911 by Isaiah Shembe, it is known colloquially as the Shembe church. The headquarters of this church are at Inanda on the outskirts of Durban, but it has many followers in rural communities, who wear distinctive beaded garments, and who worship through song and dance.

OPPOSITE: *Zulu women and children are the main inhabitants of rural areas. Even today, it is mainly the men who leave their rural homes in search of work in the cities. Many of them have the chance to return to their rural homes only at Easter and Christmas. The interiors of most rural dwellings are used for various purposes: to store food, clothing and grass mats – hung from the rafters – and to entertain guests, who are offered home-brewed beer served in fired clay pots. Some dwellings are also used to prepare the meat obtained from ritually slaughtered animals.*

THE NDEBELE

The Ndebele are well known for their outstanding craftsmanship, their decorative

homes, and their distinctive and highly colourful mode of dress and ornamentation.

They were once part of the Nguni-speaking peoples who settled along southern

Africa's eastern coastal plain, but broke away some three centuries ago and migrated

to the central inland plateau. The Ndzundza Ndebele today mainly live in the former

homeland of KwaNdebele in Mpumalanga, and around Nebo (Northern Province).

In the 17th century, the Ndebele broke away from their coastal Nguni cousins, who were to become part of the mighty Zulu empire. Under the leadership of Musi, the Ndebele migrated inland, establishing themselves north of present-day Pretoria. Musi is said to have been an astute ruler, whose first concern was the well-being of his subjects and their protection against exploitation by more powerful neighbours. Musi relied on diplomacy and not aggression to get his way. As a just and respected ruler with a gentle disposition, he is thought to have gained the confidence of the Sotho peoples among whom he and his people settled.

When Musi died, his eldest son, Manala, was named as the future chief. This was challenged by another senior son, Ndzundza, and the resulting squabble between the two divided the once united Ndebele. Eventually war became inevitable and, in a bloody struggle, Ndzundza was defeated and put to flight. He and his followers headed eastwards, settling in the upper part of the Steelpoort River basin at a place called KwaSimkhulu, near present-day Belfast, and Manala was installed as chief of his father's domain. However, it was not long before two other factions, led by other sons, broke away from the Ndebele core. The Kekana faction moved northwards and settled in the region of present-day Zebediela, and the other section, under Dlomo, returned to the east coast from where the Ndebele had originally come.

By the middle of the 19th century, the Kekana faction had further divided into smaller splinter groups, which spread out across the hills, valleys and plains surrounding present-day Potgietersrus, Zebediela and Pietersburg. These groups were progressively absorbed into the numerically superior and more dominant surrounding Sotho groups, and underwent considerable cultural change. By contrast, the descendants of Manala and Ndzundza maintained a distinctive cultural identity, and also retained their original language. The house-painting, beadwork and ornamentation often spoken of as Ndebele are in fact mostly produced by the Ndzundza Ndebele of the former southern Transvaal, and it is to these people that this chapter is primarily devoted.

By the 1820s, evidence suggests that there were Ndzundza homesteads widely dispersed along the Steelpoort. This scatter of homesteads was due in part to raids by Mzilikazi and his followers, but also to factional conflict after the death of Chief Magodongo. From the 1840s, white farmers (Boers), who had been migrating into the Highveld in growing numbers since the 1830s, started to encroach on the areas occupied by the Ndzundza Ndebele. Boer settlements sprang up between the Olifants and Steelpoort rivers, but the proximity of these towns to the chiefly stronghold of Konomtjharhelo, established by the Ndzundza regent Mabhoko I, proved irksome to Boer and Ndzundza alike. Boer attempts to subdue the chiefdom failed. Following three consecutive unsuccessful confrontations, some of which combined Swazi and Boer forces, some Boers left the area in despair, while others recognized the authority of Mabhoko and even paid tribute to him. In the late 1860s and 1870s, Ndzundza power was at its height in the region.

After 1877, with the British annexation of the Transvaal and the 1879 defeat of the Pedi by the British, the balance of power shifted away from African independent kingdoms in the region.

In the autumn of 1883 war broke out between the Boers and the Ndzundza under Nyabela, and a strategy of siege and attrition was staged by the Boers under Commandant Piet Joubert. For eight months, Nyabela and those Ndzundza who had left their dispersed settlements along the Steelpoort to group around him were besieged at Konomtjharhelo. A Boer myth has it that they were hidden in a

Top: *The Ndzundza Ndebele are well known for their geometric mural decorations.* ***Opposite:*** *An Ndebele woman with a new version of headgear. Her beaded necklace and brass neck rings are clip-on and removable, in contrast to the* iindzila *which in the past were permanently fastened around a woman's neck.*

centralized fortress of interlocking caverns, but recent evidence suggests that the well-armed Ndzundza were dug into a series of fortified settlements which spread over a much wider area. The destruction of Ndebele crops and the seizing of their cattle were largely the undoing of the chiefdom, whose people were gradually starved into submission. In July Nyabela surrendered and left his capital for the last time, as the victorious Boers torched it behind him. The conditions imposed by the victors on the vanquished were very harsh. Nyabela and other members of the chiefly family were imprisoned, and all Ndzundza lands were confiscated and given on a first-come first-served basis to the Boers who had participated in the siege. Victorious Boers were similarly favoured by being given first pick of the Ndzundza as indentured farm servants. This meant that the Ndzundza were scattered widely over the southern regions of the Transvaal Republic, including the districts of Lydenburg, Middelburg, Standerton and Wakkerstroom.

BELOW AND BOTTOM LEFT: The dolls that are sold at roadside stalls and craft shops are a major aspect of Ndebele beadwork nowadays.
BOTTOM RIGHT: An older, rarer style of apron which is predominantly white, with a small motif of coloured beads. These were worn to weddings and other ceremonial occasions (tyogolo).

The extended homesteads (*umuzi*) of the Ndzundza had been split into small, scattered family groups, but many people began to flee the farms where they had been stationed to rejoin their families on others. There were strenuous attempts to reconstruct the chieftainship (despite Nyabela's imprisonment) and to revive institutions such as initiation. By 1886, several royals had escaped from prison, instructed by Nyabela to return and 'look after his people'. They had also been charged with the duty of holding an initiation school (*wela*). On the farm Kafferskraal, not far from the old capital, they did this, to the amazement of Boer officials. A chiefdom, with no land and which no longer existed, was staging an initiation, three years after its total destruction!

Far from causing the annihilation of Ndzundza culture, this almost century-long diaspora provided the formative conditions for many social and cultural features now regarded as typically Ndebele. Some were partly borrowed from the neighbouring Pedi, but moulded by Ndebele while they lived on white farms. Ndzundza boys' initiation resembled its Pedi counterpart in being centrally controlled by the chief rather than being dispersed to separate homesteads like the more typical Nguni pattern. This countered the effects of Ndebele dispersal to white farms, allowing the chief to maintain his power despite great distance between his subjects. The Ndzundza painting style was likewise based on a Pedi original, but developed its characteristic form in the 1940s while Ndzundza lived on white farms.

RELIGION AND BELIEFS

As with most traditional groups in Africa, Ndebele life is characterized by an active spiritual world, which exercises great influence over even the smallest issues in daily existence. Illness and bad luck, good health and fortune are all seen as the result of either direct interventions from the spirit world, or the manipulations of interlocutors with that world. The latter are the healers who work for good, or witches who weave evil about them. The ancestors (abezimu), the most important denizens of the spirit world, are both solicitous and jealous, requiring constant placation through sacrifice. Failure to follow the dictates of the law and custom, as demanded by the ancestors, is believed to be the main cause of bad luck. They are also believed to protect the living against

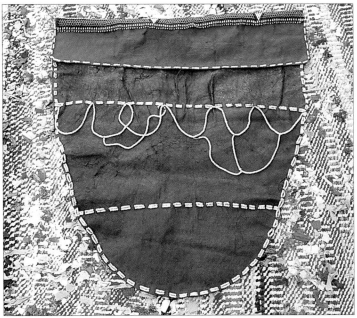

THIS PAGE: Ndebele beadwork on leather. The influences of geometric shapes deriving from building forms are in evidence in some of these designs. PAGES 68 AND 69: Older married women wearing head-rings and permanent copper or brass neck-rings (iindzila), which have been known to cause malformation of the bones in the neck. When women pay a visit to hospital, these rings are often removed, and women are reluctant to replace them.

misfortune by counselling them in dreams, and by giving strength to medicinal preparations made from herbs and other concoctions. The ancestors are thus the foundation on which traditional healing rests. The power of ancestor belief and worship has endowed the Ndebele with their cultural continuity, which has enabled them to retain a separate identity in the midst of more powerful and dominant neighbouring groupings, as well as through the ravages of war and their diaspora.

GENDER DIVISION

Strongly patriarchal attitudes and practices are evident in Ndebele communities. More than many other groups, Ndzundza men – especially those of chiefly background – continue to practise polygyny. The power

and authority of patriarchs owe something to the period these people spent as labour tenants on white farms. Demands for family labour were channelled through the male head, which bolstered his authority.

With the move away from the white farms, many men started their own businesses as taxi drivers or builders, in contrast to working on the mines or in industry as their Pedi neighbours had been doing for many years (see page 136). The women from KwaNdebele would work for years as domestic servants in Pretoria and then return home to set up

BELOW: Mrs. Francina Ndimande (seated) at her cousin's graduation. Mrs. Ndimande is an Ndebele artist who has been to many parts of the world to paint. She travelled to Scotland in 1997 to paint the Commonwealth bus. **RIGHT:** *Women wearing the traditional beaded blanket (kombers). The married woman in the centre has the long beaded ornament known as* inyoka. **OPPOSITE, TOP:** *The modern clip-on necklaces which can be removed.* **OPPOSITE, BOTTOM:** *The older, permanent necklaces.*

a homestead and look after children while being supported by their husbands. Making and selling beadwork, mats, dolls and other crafts have also provided some Ndebele women with an independent livelihood – both those who have become internationally famous like Esther Mahlangu, and those with humbler aspirations.

INITIATION AND THE RITES OF PASSAGE

Initiation is still practised among both males and females in Ndebele society, marking the passage from childhood to adult status. At the conclusion of the rites, the initiate is allowed to become sexually active and to begin the protracted process of engagement and marriage. An important function of initiation is to bond age groups together, and to

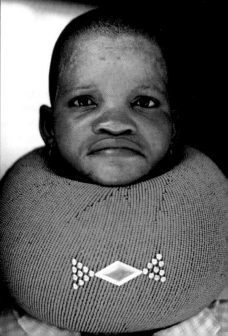

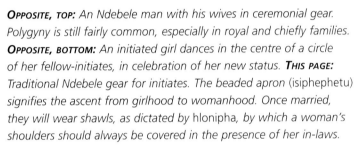

distinguish them from other age groups. Male initiates (abakhethua) are impressed upon to associate only with other men who have gone through the initiation process. In order to ensure the exclusivity and elitism of initiation, the abakhethua are instructed not to reveal to uninitiated boys what happens during the seclusion in the initiation lodge (umphadu). Through the process of initiation, males and females are inducted into traditional lore and the deep mysteries of the group. This knowledge is passed on from one generation of initiates to the next, ensuring that the transfer of knowledge is maintained, and the cultural solidarity of the group reinforced.

Male initiation (wela or ingoma) is conducted among the Ndzundza Ndebele roughly every four years, and the boys are usually 15 to 18 years old. Their names have to be registered with the paramount chief (king). Once this is done and the chief has set a date, the initiate dons a grass headband (isonyana), which indicates that he is an initiate in preparation. At this stage, he performs various ritual tasks for three weeks. Before leaving for the chief's residence, where the abakhethua from nearby homesteads meet, each is given an isititirimba (loincloth, from the Afrikaans stertriem), made for them by their grandfathers from an animal skin, and a single, often threadbare, blanket, despite the fact that initiation usually takes place during the coldest part of winter. At the chief's residence, the initiates conduct rituals, symbolically bidding farewell to their boyhood. After this, they are taken to the chief's cattle enclosure. At dawn, they are woken and taken down to a sacred place at a nearby river. They are dispersed along the river bank,

and circumcised. From here they have to cross the river (ukuwela) and march with downcast eyes under escort to different initiation lodges, depending on their village of origin. The initiates remain in the lodges, deep in the bush, for two months, being instructed on the lore of the group and their responsibilities, duties and rights as men.

After their period of seclusion, feasts are prepared at the abakhethua's homes, and the presents they receive from family members, to celebrate the attainment of manhood, are displayed. When the abakhethua leave the umphadu, it is set alight with the blankets and garments they wore during initiation, signifying the completion of their rites of passage and the closing of a chapter in their lives. After this, they return at sunset to the chief's residence, tightly wrapped in new blankets, with their eyes downcast in an obvious display of humility, similar to when they departed for the initiation lodge. Beneath their blankets the boys are naked with the exception of the isititirimba, which symbolizes manhood. That night they sleep in the enclosure and at dawn the next morning all initiates are publicly paraded (ukupalala) and officially receive their regimental names from the chief. After this, the members of the group return to their homes and a long round of celebrations.

The next stage in the young men's lives opens up as the process of engagement and marriage is contemplated, during which they are allowed to indulge in restricted sexual intercourse.

Female initiation (iqhude or ukuthombisa) is less painful than male initiation, as no clitoridectomy or body mutilations are performed. The process begins once the girl has reached puberty, starting the morning before the first full moon, when the girls are stripped naked and symbolically returned to nature, by having all the hair on their bodies shaved off. Each initiate is attended by appointed guides – older girls and women who have been initiated. Once the girls are prepared, the rest of the day is spent singing and dancing to the accompaniment of a drum-like instrument, from which a twanging sound is produced. In the evening, the girls gather around a fire, wearing a blanket given to them for initiation, while the guides are stripped naked. They sing songs before launching into a tirade of abuse and cursing against males, the concept of masculinity and male sexual organs, and women who have not been initiated. This ritual abuse lasts throughout the

OPPOSITE LEFT, TOP AND BOTTOM: Young men at initiation, waiting for the chief to let them out of the enclosure. Those in the picture at the top have staffs and are wearing the 'Middelburg blanket' with its broad, coloured stripes; those in the bottom picture are dressed only in isititirimba *(leather loincloths).* **OPPOSITE RIGHT, TOP:** *An Ndebele chief dressed in royal leopard-skin apparel, to welcome young men from the initiation.* **OPPOSITE RIGHT, MIDDLE AND BOTTOM:** *Boys dressed up and ready for celebration.* **ABOVE:** *Father welcoming his son from initiation.* **TOP RIGHT:** *The new wardrobe* (isogana) *for the initiate is displayed for all to see.*

night. Early the next morning, the initiates and their guides go to a river, where the former are ritually washed, after which they return to their homesteads. The next day a celebration is held and the initiate is again washed. She then goes into seclusion in a specially constructed room in her own home. In earlier times the period of seclusion was three months, but today, with the demands of schooling and employment, it has been reduced to one month. During this time, the initiate receives instruction from her guides. She is also visited by the grandmothers of the homestead, who instruct her on lore and customs, as

well as her duties and responsibilities. The main point of initiation, however, is to instruct the initiate on the duties and practices of home-making. During her seclusion, she is not allowed to talk to or see any males, and thus she performs the domestic duties she is taught during initiation at night or in the early hours of the morning.

At the end of the seclusion, the initiate is taken to the river for a final washing. Her initiation blanket and clothes are burnt, symbolizing the 'death' of girlhood. She is given an *isiphephetu*, a stiff beaded apron, as a sign of her ascent from girlhood to womanhood. As with male initiation, the changed status of the initiate is celebrated with communal feasting in succession at the homes of all the girls who underwent initiation. This is a time of joy, during which the newly initiated women are able to flirt and attract the attention of a potential husband.

ART AND BEADWORK

The Ndzundza Ndebele are best known for their art. Similar motifs, designs and colours are used in mural decoration (done by the women) and beadwork. Patterns embrace a variety of forms and symbols: elaborate use is made of geometric shapes, and natural objects such as flowers, snakes, birds and small animals. In modern times, letters of the

ABOVE: *Traditional healers dancing at their graduation ceremony. The healer in front is carrying the dancing stick.* **LEFT:** *An Ndebele bride is not allowed to be seen by outsiders; however hot the day may be, she will cover her face at all times with the blanket she is wearing. She will be led by a person holding an umbrella over her.*

alphabet, numerals, representations of urban buildings, windmills and aeroplanes are used. The early Ndebele relied on natural pigments (soot, ash and clay) for the colours in their decorations. With the arrival of white traders, however, they had access to a wide range of coloured paints, which are extensively used today. Traditionally, women devoted their time to mural art in the late autumn and winter months, when the planting, weeding and harvesting of sorghum and maize crops were completed, and they had a reasonable amount of leisure time. This is also the time of the year when they did most of their beadwork, sitting together in their courtyards of their homes, enjoying the camaraderie of other women in the homestead and the mellow warmth of the winter sun. Beadwork, however, was not exclusively a winter activity, as it was also done during free moments in summer and spring.

It is a moot point whether the elaborate personal adornment worn by Ndebele women owes more to their own aesthetic sensibilities or to the wishes of Ndebele men to have their status as wealthy husbands displayed by their wives' ornamentation. The range of ornaments worn, which become increasingly spectacular after marriage and with age, is probably greater than that of any other grouping. The *iirholwana*, beaded wire hoops of various sizes which are worn by women around their wrists, arms, ankles, legs, neck and stomach, are probably the most popular. In earlier times, once her home was built, an Ndebele wife would also wear copper or brass rings *(iindzila)* around her neck. These are believed to have strong ritual powers, although wearing them on a permanent basis is no longer common practice. Often, an older woman who wears these rings will have them removed on a visit to hospital, after which they will not be replaced. Traditionally the husband provided his wife with her *iindzila*; the more rings she wore, the greater was her husband's wealth reputed to be. *Iindzila* are considered by a wife to be a token of her bond with and faithfulness to her husband. Only on his death would she remove them.

Among both the Manala and Ndzundza, girls wear ornaments from early childhood. These comprise beaded anklets, wristlets and necklaces. At this age, they traditionally wear loin coverings *(iinrhabi)*, little cascades of leather thongs attached to waist-straps and tipped with beads, which cover the upper part of the thighs. In adolescence, instead of the *iinrhabi*, the *isiphephetu* is worn, a small, rectangular

and stiffly beaded fore-apron. After marriage, this is replaced with the *umaphotho*, a large, goat-skin apron, which often reaches the ankles and is intricately decorated with white beads. On her wedding day, the bride wears a veil of threaded beads which completely hides her face.

Traditionally the colours of the beads were endowed with special significance, reflecting the stages of development in a person's life, from infancy to parenthood. The combination of colours also reflected the mood of the maker: joy, happy expectation, sorrow, or insecurity. With urbanization and modernization, this has largely disappeared.

Ndebele men seldom adorn themselves, except for rituals and ceremonies, when they wear what has been given to them by their wives.

BELOW: *Two Ndebele women travelling to a wedding, both adorned in their colourful ceremonial gear.* **PAGE 78,** AND **PAGE 79** TOP: *Mrs. Francina Ndimande's homestead, with children being taught Ndebele wall-painting.* **PAGE 79,** BOTTOM: *Esther Mahlangu has become internationally renowned as a painter and decorator.*

OPPOSITE, TOP: *The Weltevrede Roman Catholic church next to the royal homestead has been decorated by Mrs. Francina Ndimande.* **OPPOSITE, BOTTOM:** *This homestead in the former KwaNdebele was abandoned in the late 1980s by its owner, Chief Eli Masemula.* **ABOVE:** *Esther Mahlangu with the BMW she was commissioned to paint.*

RECENT DEVELOPMENTS

Being dispersed as servants on white farms was not the only major experience of upheaval in the lives of the Ndzundza. Another significant disruption came almost a century later, when large-scale changes in white agriculture caused the Ndebele farm tenants to be put under ever-increasing pressure. In some cases, the farmer would mechanize and, no longer requiring the service of semi-feudal labourers, would simply evict the family. In other cases, the farmer gradually increased the amount of time which young men had to spend working on the farm, causing many Ndzundza sons to run away. With the family no

longer able to fulfil its labour service, the man's parents and sisters would then be driven off the farms, and the family as a whole would have to find a new place to live. Both of these scenarios saw numbers of Ndzundza – often accompanied by the herds of cattle they had built up – looking for new places to settle. They moved either to the newly formed homeland of KwaNdebele or to the older (Northern Sotho) homeland of Lebowa.

Many critics saw KwaNdebele as the ultimate 'dumping ground', and regarded its 'Chief Minister' and his sinister henchmen as stooges of the apartheid government. But it was to be the scene of an incident hardly less dramatic or definitive than the Boer–Ndebele War of 1883. During the darkest days of apartheid, in the late 1980s, there erupted a wave of popular resistance, supported by the then ruling Ndzundza king, against the repressive officials of the KwaNdebele government. Such was the support enjoyed by this uprising that it successfully quelled all suggestions of KwaNdebele 'independence' under apartheid. The Ndebele had shown, and continue to show, that traditionalism is not as rigid as it might appear, and that royalist attitudes can be invoked in the service of a representative democracy.

THE VENDA

Venda culture has arisen from diverse origins. Many Venda see themselves as

traditionalists, but their culture has been very dynamic and adaptable. In the past,

they controlled a vast area in the north of the country. Today, as a result of land

seizure by whites in the late 19th and early 20th centuries, and the apartheid policies

from the 1960s, they are centred in the north-east, mainly around Louis Trichardt and

Sibasa in Northern Province. Groups are also found in south-eastern Zimbabwe.

Fanciful theories have been used to explain the origins of the Venda, but recent evidence has revealed them to be an amalgam of groups. By the fourth century, modern Northern Province was occupied by Khoisan and Early Iron Age peoples, who interacted through trade, marriage and war. In the 7th century the northern reaches were occupied by Ngona and Khoisan. From 800, the Mapungubwe Kingdom emerged, stretching from the Soutpansberg in the south, across the Limpopo River to the Matopos in the north. The kingdom declined from 1240, and the centre of power and trade moved north to the Great Zimbabwe Kingdom. A shifting of focus to Zimbabwe's Khami and Rozwi empires followed, but culture did not come to a standstill south of the Limpopo: Shona-Venda and Venda pottery styles developed in the 14th and 15th centuries. There are no stone-walled ruins comparable in size to Great Zimbabwe in the north-eastern part of Northern Province, but those in the mountains do show the link.

Accompanying the emergence of these centres, from about 1400, waves of Shona-speaking migrants from modern Zimbabwe (known by the Venda as Thavatsindi) settled across the Lowveld. At the end of the 17th century, another wave, the Singo, probably of Rozwi origin, fled Danangombe (Dhlo Dhlo) near the centre of Zimbabwe, on the break-up of the Rozwi empire. They settled first at Tshiendeulu, and then Dzata.

A drum, *Ngoma Lungundu* (the drum of the dead or of Mwari), is a central feature of oral traditions about the Singo: if beaten by the king in times of threat, it would protect the people against attack and allow them to defeat their enemies. The drum struck such fear into enemies' souls that they fled in terror, fell to the ground in a swoon, or died. Tradition has it that the drum enabled the Singo to undertake their journey and occupy and hold land south of the Limpopo. At times, when the drum appeared to play itself, the invisible ancestor-god Mwari, who had given the drum to the Singo kings, himself was playing it.

Dzata in the Nzhelele Valley has extensive stone walling, and for some 60 years had a succession of rulers. Most accounts of its history centre around Thoho-ya-Ndou (Head of the Elephant), who may have been

several rulers who took the name on accession to the throne. Some accounts portray him as the man who united Soutpansberg groups to form the Venda. Others say he extended Venda power and boundaries to incorporate neighbouring groups.

In 1760, Dzata burnt to the ground. The fate of Thoho-ya-Ndou is a mystery: he may have fled, with the *Ngoma Lungundu*, to settle across the Limpopo, or he may have been murdered. Some accounts state that the drum was hidden in a cave near Netshiendeulu, whose inhabitants were its keepers.

With the disappearance of Thoho-ya-Ndou, the kingdom was divided in two. Secessions in the 19th century resulted in even more groups, whose *mahosi* (kings) all claim Singo descent. The Venda also had *mahosi* of other origins. Laws about succession to the throne are complex, and Venda history has been characterized by frequent succession disputes, which persist to the present.

Although living among the Venda, the Lemba retain traits (such as avoiding pork) that show their distinct origins. Some argue that the Lemba of Northern Province and Zimbabwe are descendants of Arab traders who ranged between East Africa and the Zimbabwean plateau centuries ago. The Lemba themselves believe they are Black Jews, descendants of the lost tribe of Israel. Whatever their origins, they played an important role as carriers of goods in precolonial iron and gold trading. In the past, no Lemba woman could marry a Venda man, and marriage of Lemba men with Venda women was rare. Should a Venda woman marry a Lemba, she had to undergo a ceremony to become a Lemba. This still pertains, at least in theory, today.

Trade, warfare and intermarriage with Tsonga, Lobedu, Zulu, Swazi and other people have also left their imprints on Venda culture.

TOP: A young girl singing at the dombani *initiation school.* **OPPOSITE:** *Girls taking part in the* dombani, *wearing cloths called* vhulungu ka na ludede. *The girl playing the* mirumba *is wearing a* shedu *(small apron).*

ABOVE: *Initiates around* Nyamuthenga, *the old woman (or man) in charge of the* dombani. **OPPOSITE, TOP AND BOTTOM LEFT:** *Girls perform the* domba *dance accompanied by* ngoma *and* mirumba *drums.* **OPPOSITE, BOTTOM RIGHT:** *A lesson in* u losha *(to salute or honour). Losha varies according to sex and the position of the person performing it.*

POLITICAL ORGANIZATION

Elements of traditional political organization still exist in rural areas. The smallest unit is the household *(mudi)*, a family or a group of families of the same lineage, who live together in a collection of rondavels. The *mudi* is under a *mukoma*, the father of the *mudi*'s most important family. Succession to *mukoma* is usually hereditary, but formal approval must be given by the *khosi* (king) of the subgroup to which the *mudi* belongs. The *mukoma* is responsible for order and government in the *mudi*. His jurisdiction is confined to petty cases between members of the *mudi*, and his privileges are restricted to the right to expect obedience, free labour and tribute from members of his *mudi*. In judicial duties he is assisted by his council *(khoro)*. Procedure is informal, and there is no voting: after discussion on a subject is exhausted, the *mukoma* reaches a decision and passes a verdict, which accords with majority feeling. Should he oppose the *khoro*, he will try to persuade them to his viewpoint. Failing this, the matter is referred to higher authority. This has seldom happened, as the Venda system is flexible and characterized by a strong desire to avoid confrontation.

Several units *(midi)* form a *kavhelo* under a headman, whose privileges, duties and powers are similar to a *mukoma*'s, on a larger scale. He is assisted by councils of heads of the *midi*, and older men from his own *mudi*. A *lushaka*, people from various districts, under the authority of the same *khosi*, is the third tier, the largest political unit in Venda society.

Today, traditional villages with stone walls may be found nestling under cliffs. Typically the king is at the highest part of the village, with his wives and family in front of him. Others occupy the lower and surrounding areas, protecting the *khosi* and his wives. The entrance to the king's residential section is adjacent to the *khoro* (public court); access to the ruler, particularly by strangers, is limited. After permission has been granted to see him, subjects are taken through winding passages and up steps to the large rondavel that is the meeting place.

Traditionally, a king had great power and influence, his secular authority grounded in spiritual might. He approached the ancestors on behalf of the nation; this marked the apex of a pyramid in which the *mukoma* could approach the ancestors on behalf of the household.

It used to be thought that the king was the high priest, but now we understand the position better. In traditional society, the very young and old were accorded great respect and honour: the young were still close to the ancestors, and the old about to re-join them and become ancestors themselves. As an extension of this, the *khosi* was a living ancestor. He had to be approached on hands and knees; he addressed everyone with condescension in the second person singular, but he had to be addressed in the polite third person plural. Distinction was also made between the king and his people in naming objects and actions associated with the king. For example, if the king were drunk, people would say he had 'fallen into a pool of water'. People would not refer to a king's death directly, but would say, 'the pool has no more water'. The language spoken in his *musanda* (royal capital) was highly symbolic and differed from that spoken by commoners. Because he was considered semi-divine, he was lauded for anything he did, no matter how mundane – coughing, drinking beer, even expectorating. It was not unusual for a king, as he grew old, to perform a solemn solitary dance *(u pembela)*, which turned him into a god *(Mudzimu)*. The *khosi*, though powerful, was not a tyrannical despot and had to operate within the laws and customs of society. Only in rare circumstances could he deviate, and this had to be sanctioned by his council. *Mahosi* were powerless, within taboo and ritual, to make alterations without the sanction of the people. Some rituals were overseen by *khosi*'s principal sister *(makhadzi)*, who ensured that tradition was followed. In the past kings were assisted in their functions by a council of the *magota* and *dzinduna*, as well as the *vhakoma* (brothers and cousin-brothers of the king) who lived nearest his palace or Great Place. Kings who tried to deviate too far from established tradition ran the risk of being poisoned by the wider royal family or having their subjects 'vote with their feet' and move away to the area of authority of another ruler.

INITIATION

As with other southern Africa peoples, Venda initiation played an important educational role. The development of the individual was seen as a series of phases, puberty and marriage marking important stages. Transition from one to the next was made possible by external forces (the ancestors, good and evil spirits, witches of both sexes), which could exert good or bad influences on people. Initiation schools instructed initiates about what to expect and how to behave in the next stage. Through ceremonies and dances, they could break with the mistakes of the past and embrace the future. The ceremonies also invoked the support of the ancestors and strengthened the initiates through magic. Held at, or near, the villages of *mahosi* and *magota* when there were sufficient participants, they did not necessarily occur every year.

ABOVE: *Initiates* losha *to Nyamuthenga. In the past, the Venda wore skin clothing, but with increasing trade last century the* minwenda *(the garment under her towel) became 'traditional' female dress.*

A Venda girl attends three major initiation schools: *vhusha* at puberty; *tshikanda*, to reinforce the *vhusha*; and *dombani*, a pre-marital school.

In the past, boys who had been through the *thondo* also attended parts of the *dombani*, but today very few do, and the boys' schools, *vhutuka* and *thondo*, are obsolete. Most attend *murundu*, introduced at a later stage. It takes place outside the village, usually on a hill or mountain, in the dry winter months, to aid in the healing of the circumcision wound. These days, an increasing number, particularly in urban areas, are circumcised by Western doctors, rather than traditional specialists. Some of these doctors have developed ceremonies of their own and slaughter a beast after a number of people have been circumcised, to give the operation some form of 'traditional' legitimacy.

The *vhusha* used to last several months, but today it often takes place over only eight days. Girls are taught that humility is the essence of Venda womanhood. While secluded at a lodge, they assume a bearing of abject subservience, keeping their heads bowed, their shoulders stooped and arms folded, or their hands cupped under their chins. They perform menial tasks, bearing heavy loads on their backs or heads, wriggling on their stomachs, or holding embers in their hands. They are given extensive education on sex, sexual behaviour, betrothal and marriage, and avoiding pregnancy outside marriage.

Distinction was traditionally made between *vhusha* of daughters of nobles (*vhusha ha vhakololo*) and commoners (*vhusha ha vhasiwana*). Singing, dancing and learning the *milayo* were important features of the school for commoners. The school for nobles was more secret, and little is known about it. Almost all its activities took place within a secluded enclosure at the chief's village, and there was no music to announce publicly that the school was being held. No commoner could attend the nobles' *vhusha*, but nobles who had already undergone *vhusha* could visit the commoners' *vhusha* whenever they wished.

The *tshikanda* took place just before the *dombani*, every three or four years. The *dombani*, marking the culmination of the initiation process, was the final qualification for marriage. The blowing of a kudu horn (*phala phala*) marked the start. A sacred fire, lit at the king's village, remained alight throughout. The initiates were treated with medicines, and everything used was sprinkled with medicine to prevent evil interference. All initiates were shaved, and for the rest of the *dombani* were not allowed to shave or wash. Traditionally the *dombani* had 10 stages, lasting up to two years, but today seldom more than nine months. The initiates are taught dances and secret songs, exposed to secret objects, watch and participate in teaching mimes, and receive sexual education. The objective is to acquaint the young with all aspects of marriage, as well as Venda mores. Viewed as a 'national' event by the Venda, the *dombani* can only be held under the auspices of a *khosi* of Singo descent.

A striking feature of the *dombani* is the *domba* dance performed by the girls around the sacred fire. The initiates form a line, each holding the elbow of the girl in front of her, making a long chain which weaves rhythmically to the beat of the *ngoma* and *mirumba* drums. Traditionally the girls danced naked, but today they wear the *shedu* which is passed between the legs, forming an apron in the front with a back panel hanging down. They also wear metal bracelets and anklets that glint as

BELOW: *A young woman of royal descent wearing the* minwenda *as she pounds maize* (tola mavhele). *The* tshikandwa *around her neck is associated with the ancestral spirits.* **BELOW RIGHT:** *Vhatukana vha murundu – boys coming from the mountain initiation school.*

they dance. The dance symbolizes a python, which is associated with fertility and the movements of a baby in the womb. It also represents the python believed to inhabit Fundudzi, the sacred lake of the Venda in a Soutpansberg valley. The *khoro* wall is the body of the python god, and the courtyard Lake Fundudzi, the place of origin, the cosmological womb; the initiates are thus in the womb of the python, ready to be reborn as marriageable and respectful members of society.

Christian churches adopt varying attitudes towards initiation, some forbidding members to attend initiation schools. Some 'independent' churches encourage members to attend, and others provide alternatives, usually blending traditional beliefs and practices with Christianity.

Other changes have been wrought by modern education, hospitals and migrant labour, but many girls are still initiated. In the past, no Venda man would marry a woman who had not been through *dombani*. If he married a woman from another group, such as Tsonga or Sotho, she would have to go through *dombani*. Today, the reason most initiates give for their attendance is to 'learn the laws' or 'gain wisdom' (*u guda milayo*). Knowing the *milayo* endows a woman with special knowledge which entitles her to participate in women's meetings and ceremonies.

MUSIC AND DANCE

Music and dance play a central part in Venda life, being performed at weddings and funerals, rituals and initiation schools, beer drinking and gatherings. Dance is also important in independent churches to which many Venda belong. Some musicians play popular and religious music, but traditional forms are often incorporated into modern compositions.

Musical instruments, music, song and dance express status and power, and have religious significance. Many instruments that have disappeared elsewhere in Africa are still used: *mbila* (xylophone), *mbira* (thumb piano), *thsikona* (reed flutes), stringed instruments, *mirumba* (treble drums), *ngoma* (bass drums) and *thungwa* (drums like the *ngoma*, but smaller).

Kings had (and still have) a *tshikona* ensemble, whose ability reflected their power and prestige and, thus, their people's. *Ngoma* drums, one of the main symbols of kingship, in the past were played only at court.

OPPOSITE AND ABOVE: Bracelets and anklets (vhukunda tshotshane *and* vhukunda ha mulenzhe)*, which are worn proudly by women, are given to a bride by her husband's family to mark significant events.*

Very young children are encouraged to imitate adults' songs and dances. When they are bigger, they sing children's songs *(nyimbo dza vhana)*: *nyimbo*, simple jingles that are sung during the day, and *ngano*, during the evening, especially at harvest *(mavhuya-haya)*. The latter are story songs, often performed by adults and children of both sexes.

Dzhombo, characterized by display and erotic action, takes place on moonlit nights at *mavhuya-haya*. Girls and boys face each other and, accompanied by clapping, dance in turn between the lines. The dancer touches a person of the opposite sex to show a preference. The songs are rhythmic and melodic and more complex than *nyimbo* and *ngano*.

The main dances performed by young people before marriage are *tshikanganga* and *tshigombela*. They are an important part of life, but evidence suggests they are not very old. The *tshikanganga* is a fast dance in which boys play reed-flutes and girls accompany them on *thungwa* and *mirumba* drums. It is performed for pleasure, but permission must be obtained from the headman or king. The *tshigombela*, for girls, occurs before harvest. Accompanied by one *thungwa* and two *mirumba* drums, a girl begins a song and others join in the chorus; they dance anti-clockwise around the drums, the pitch of the song rising.

The *malombo* dance is the second phase of treatment for a person (usually female) possessed by a homeless spirit *(tshilombo)*. If a woman falls ill and a diviner indicates the presence of a *tshilombo*, special treatment is necessary. In the first phase, a specialist *(maine a tshele)* brings the woman into a trance, causes her to collapse, treats her with medicines and asks the spirit to identify itself and its wishes. The spirit is thus introduced into the body of the afflicted woman (medium), rather than exorcized. In the second phase, the medium joins a society of *malombo* dancers of previously healed patients. The dance takes place in the *khoro*

(courtyard) of the king, who lends the society some of his instruments. The spirit is often male, and possessed women may behave like men, wear male garments (waistcoats, ties and hats) and carry male objects (imitation assegais or miniature axes). This has led to the belief that the *malombo* cult is an organized movement opposing male superiority.

SCULPTURE

Until relatively recently, wood-carving was largely limited to a few utensils (dishes, spoons, milk jugs and headrests) and objects for royal use (drums, exquisite doors, divining bowls, xylophones, game-boards and figurines for use in initiation schools). Many disappeared at the end of the 19th century and the beginning of this century, taken by force, robbed from graves and sacred sites, traded by early white visitors to the area, or destroyed by early missionaries. Today, there is a lively market in work produced by locals.

THE POSITION OF WOMEN

Traditionally Venda women did not have the same inferior position held by women in most southern African groups. Within her courtyard, a woman had absolute control, and in the past elderly women played an important role in education, telling their stories around the fire. Women could own property, usually given to them by their fathers, but it could be inherited when there was no male heir. There are cases of women acting as regent for a minor son, and a *khosi* could also appoint his sister as *nduna* or *mukoma*. At least one rulership (at Mianzwi) has been passed down in the female line for generations.

The *makhadzi*, the older sister of a household head, knew the intimate secrets of the family and had more rights over her brother's children than their mother. Many rituals could not be performed without her, and in the case of kings she played a major role in determining succession.

THE TSONGA

The Tsonga are not an homogeneous ethnic group that can trace its roots back

to a single founder. Their forefathers came from present-day Mozambique to settle

in South Africa in the 19th century, generally in small groups without

important chiefs. Today the Tsonga are centred mainly in the Lowveld between the

Escarpment and the western borders of the Kruger National Park.

The first Tsonga-speakers to enter the former Transvaal probably did so during the 18th century. They were essentially traders who followed rivers inland, where they bartered cloth and beads for ivory, copper and salt. In the early 1820s they were joined by co-linguists pushed from the coast by Nguni raiders. At this time the Tsonga living on the coastal plain constituted a loose cluster of linguistically related peoples who shared a few distinguishing customs, but had no single political identity. Their small groups could offer only limited resistance to the invading Nguni.

The last Nguni group to come to the area was a remnant of the Ndwandwe army, under Shoshangane, which had suffered a mauling at the hands of Shaka and his Zulu *impis* on the Mhlatuze River banks, near present-day Ulundi. The refugees settled along the Tembe River, south-east of what is today Swaziland, but before long they turned on the Tsonga, moving north in a gentle sweep to the Limpopo Valley. An uneasy peace developed as the Ndwandwe (or Shangaans) began to incorporate Tsonga-speakers into their ranks.

In 1828 Shaka, brooding over his unfinished battle with the Ndwandwe a decade earlier, sent his army after Shoshangane. It was his last military adventure before his assassination that year (*see page 34*). The Zulu were unable to pin Shoshangane down, and no conclusive battle was ever fought. An Nguni state on Zululand's northern border was an irritation to the Zulu, serving as a home for political dissidents and threatening the important trade route to Lourenço Marques (now Maputo). A new Zulu expedition was sent north in 1833 to attack Shoshangane and punish his allies. They seized Lourenço Marques and impaled the governor of the town on the beach. In the face of this Zulu resurgence Shoshangane and his followers fled from their settlement in the lower Limpopo Valley. They advanced to the Zambezi River before going south to settle in Mosapa (Zimbabwe). From here Shoshangane began to subdue and incorporate the Shona-speaking Ndau. Using his expanded forces, he strengthened his power over the area between the Zambezi River and Delagoa Bay. Steadily the Gaza kingdom, named in

honour of Shoshangane's grandfather who had lived in the Mkuze district of Zululand, began to emerge along the eastern edge of the escarpment and in the steamy bush of the coastal plain.

A period of relative peace ensued, during which the Ndwandwe from the south and the Tsonga, who had been in the region for centuries, steadily influenced each other. This was intensified after 1838, when many of Shoshangane's soldiers died in a smallpox epidemic, and he moved back to the Limpopo Valley His troups devastated the area, as he punished his enemies, enslaved women and children, and demanded heavy payments of tribute. This turmoil dislodged two streams of refugees from the coastal plain. The Nkuna and other small groups moved west along the Olifants River to place themselves under the Sotho-speaking Kaha and Lovedu on the western Lowveld. A second wave of refugees (Maluleke, Baloyi, Tshauke and Sono) followed the Limpopo to settle along the Levubu (Pafuri) River or in the lowlands to the east of the Soutpansberg and Drakensberg. Small bands of refugees retained their chiefs by settling in inhospitable, malarial areas but, if they wished to live around the healthier highlands they had to seek the protection of leaders like the Sotho-speaking Modjadji, Podile and Maake in the south or the Venda-speaking Pafuri in the north. In the 1850s Tsonga immigrants made their home in the Spelonken foothills of the Soutpansberg where a Portuguese adventurer, João Albasini, was building a personal kingdom out of profits made from the sale of slaves and ivory. But, while the Tsonga refugees in the interior started to form small communities, their kinsmen on the coast had to withstand continuing political upheavals.

Top: Elderly women are respectfully called kokwana *(grandmothers).*
Opposite: Geometrical patterns decorate the walls of this enclosure. A homestead will often include cylindrical dwellings with thatched cone roofs, as well as square houses roofed in corrugated iron.

TOP LEFT: *A gate in the perimeter wall of the homestead leads to the central courtyard.* **MIDDLE:** *A small granary on stilts allows air to circulate, keeping cereals dry.* **ABOVE:** *The design of this enclosure (freshly painted after the harvest) is typically Tsonga, based on the shape of the mortar in which maize is crushed.* **TOP RIGHT:** *An earth shelf, built into the wall of the dwelling, provides seating.*

In 1858 Shoshangane died and the kingdom began to disintegrate as his sons, Muzila and Mawewe, locked horns over the throne. Shoshangane had named Muzila as successor, which Mawewe contested; this led to almost 10 years of continuous fighting. Aided by Albasini and traders at Lourenço Marques, Muzila gained the upper hand. Mawewe fled to Swaziland, where he sought the help of King Mswati I, finally settling in northern Swaziland on the border with Gazaland. Muzila had shifted the centre of the Gaza state back to the safety of Mosapa, leaving the Delagoa Bay hinterland unprotected. Each winter the Swazi launched devastating raids into the area. In 1884 Muzila died and his son, Gungunyana, succeeded him. The new king rapidly tried to re-establish control over southern Gazaland. In 1889 he moved his capital to the lower Limpopo, colonizing the southern reaches of his empire. The ensuing disruption initiated a new wave of immigration into the Transvaal and brought Gungunyana into conflict with the Portuguese.

As the natural port for the Witwatersrand, Lourenço Marques had grown with the newly discovered gold fields. This gave the Portuguese the desire and means to establish control over southern Mozambique; in 1895 an expedition from Lisbon defeated Gungunyana and exiled him to the Azores. His son, Thulilamahanxi, then a minor, and the regent, Mpisane, fled to the Transvaal Republic and settled north of the Sabi River along the foothills of the Drakensberg mountain range, in the present district of Mhala.

The crushing of the Gaza was completed two years later when an uprising led by one of Gungunyana's generals was mercilessly subdued. This initiated a new wave of emigration as the remnants of the Gaza empire crossed the border and entered the Transvaal. In 1910 Mpisane renounced his regency in favour of Thulilamahanxi, who was recognized by the family council as heir in the absence of the still exiled Buyisonto, the legitimate successor to Gungunyana. In 1922 Buyisonto came out of exile and moved to Mhala to become the leader of the descendants of the old Gaza kingdom.

By this time Tsonga-speakers constituted about 4 percent of the total South African population. In the Transvaal they lived in distinct areas. In the north, quite large chiefdoms, such as those of Xikundu, Mhinga, Xigalo and Makuleke, occupied reserves adjoining or near the Kruger National Park. Further south, scattered communities eked out a

living in the Lowveld. Near the headwaters of the Levubu and Small Letaba rivers, Christian converts stayed on Swiss Mission farms at Valdezia, Elim and Kurulen, their children attending the celebrated Lemana College. Further south, the Nkuna and several small groups lived on the edge of the Escarpment. The descendants of the Nguni-speaking Shangaans, with their Tsonga-speaking wives and followers, occupied the land between Acornhoek–Bushbuckridge and the southern end of the Kruger Park. Probably the largest single group of Tsonga-speakers was in the Ingwavuma–Ubombo districts of northern Zululand. These were the descendants of the Maputo (Mabudhu in Zulu), whose kingdom was cut in two by the border between South Africa and Mozambique. Unlike the Tsonga in the Transvaal, they had close ties with the Zulu.

SOCIAL ORGANIZATION

In the 1890s Lowveld farms were suitable for little more than hunting and subsistence agriculture, and the owners soon sold them to specu-lators looking for mineral deposits. Tsonga-speakers in the area paid rent to the absent speculators; where owners worked the land, tenants paid in kind (often half the harvested crop) or labour (as much as six months per year). As land prices rose, and large parts of the Lowveld were cleared of malaria and sleeping-sickness, tenants were forced to become contracted labourers or leave the farm. Restricted by pass laws from moving to cities, many families settled on land reserved for African occupation. But they were again moved as 'betterment' cam-paigns in the 1940s sought to consolidate scattered homesteads into large villages, erect fencing and separate arable from cultivable land.

In the 1960s and 1970s communities were torn apart as families were moved to the Tsonga 'homeland', Gazankulu. Taxation and over-population in the reserves made people increasingly dependent on migrant labour. This caused men to leave their families for long periods, and today even women in rural areas seek seasonal work on nearby farms. Combined with the tedium of life in the villages, this long assault on the structure of the family has led to many ills: alcoholism, AIDS, teenage pregnancies and unemployment are rife.

TOP LEFT: *A woman stirs maize porridge over a fire in a domestic enclosure. Tsonga immigrants introduced maize into the Transvaal Republic in the 19th century.* **TOP RIGHT:** *Cobs of maize are hung out to dry, before being pounded in an x-shaped mortar (seen in the background).* **ABOVE:** *Women making beer by sifting the grains of maize and sorghum through a home-made, wooden filter.*

It is, however, still possible to talk of a traditional Tsonga homestead *(muti)*: a typical settlement consists of a man, his wife or wives, their children and the families of their married sons. The construction of the houses, cylindrical with earth walls and conical thatched or reed roofs, reflects their Tsonga origins. While the layout of the *muti* varies from area to area, they all share certain characteristics. The homestead is generally circular with a perimeter wall or fence, made from branches and tree stumps. In the centre is the cattle byre *(xivaya* or *tshanga)* opposite the main entrance (which strangers must use) on the eastern side of the homestead. Other entrances leading to fields and water points are used by members of the *muti*. The homestead of the principal wife *(yindlu lonkulu)* is behind the *xivaya* at 12 o'clock, and those of other wives flank it. Each has her own cooking area, in a hut or an area screened by reed, stone or earth walling. The *yindlu lonkulu* has her own granary, usually a small structure raised on stilts. Children are housed separately by sex – girls well within the *muti* and boys between the main gate and the *xivaya*. A special area *(huvo)*, usually enclosed by logs and branches and situated under a tree, is used for meetings; another area *(gandzelo)*, which may be anywhere in the *muti*, is for sacrificial purposes. The *vandla*, which may be inside or outside the *muti*, is where the men meet to discuss the administration and the affairs of the *muti*. No woman or child is allowed in this area.

Authority in the family rests with the father, who is treated with great respect by his wife and children. Within an extended family, the ranking and status of wives are determined by the order in which they were married. The first wife *(nsati lonkulu)* is the principal wife; she has the highest rank and status and has to be accorded due respect by the others. Ranking and status are also accorded to the children and are determined by their mothers' standing. Rank, status, and gender determine the relationships between all siblings. In addition, rules of conduct, obligations, duties, rights and privileges exist in a code of behaviour which each child is expected to observe.

TRADITIONAL POLITICAL STRUCTURES

As white colonists imposed their rule on villages, the powers of chiefs declined. By the 1920s many whites saw in the disintegration of the chiefdom the spectre of political lawlessness. Segregationists saw the 'tribe' as the 'natural' home of an African population entering into increasing competition with whites in urban areas. The position of the chief was strengthened by legislation in the 1920s and, 30 years later, 'tribal authorities' became crucial to the Bantustan system. Traditionally the chief *(hosi)* and his council have the final authority and still form an important part of government in all Tsonga groups. Chieftainship is hereditary and falls to the most senior member of the oldest lineage in the strongest clan in the group. The new chief must be approved by the council and formally inducted into office. Should he be a minor on the death of his father, his father's younger brother normally acts as regent.

In the past the *hosi* wielded supreme power. He allocated land and sanctioned the start of initiation rites, harvest ceremonies and rain dances; he mediated between members of the group and ancestral spirits; he made all decisions relating to war and the army; he was also responsible for the administration of the group, and tried serious cases and those on appeal from headmen. He was assisted by officials who

LEFT: A man's status is enhanced by the size of his family. BELOW: A businessman, Solomon Bvuma from Xihoko, with his wives, wearing the colourful cloths introduced to the area by 19th century traders.

carried out special tasks. Today chiefs are paid civil servants responsible for administering the people under their charge. They have to collect taxes and oversee such services as the allocation of piped water or the construction of new classrooms. They continue to play an important role as centres of loyalty, identity and affection for rural communities.

EARLY LIFE IN A *MUTI*

The birth of a baby is a moment of great joy in Tsonga society. Usually older female relatives, or other wives, help pregnant mothers through the last stages of their pregnancy and the birth of the infant. Newly born babies are doctored with medicines and decorated with charms and beaded bangles. Normally mothers breast-feed for at least the first two years of their babies' lives. Once children can walk, the burden of bringing them up is shared between the mother and older sisters.

Children are expected to perform domestic duties from an early age. Daughters help their mother in their daily duties, gathering firewood, and fetching water from a nearby river, spring or tap, carrying water containers on their heads. Older boys herd the family's cattle, while the younger boys herd the goats.

In many parts of the old Transvaal adult status was attained after initiation. Boys and girls were initiated in separate groups and, only after the prescribed rites had been performed, were they allowed to marry.

ABOVE AND BELOW: *Female novices* (swikhombani) *taking part in the festivities that form part of the ceremony which marks their initiation from girlhood to womanhood.*

ABOVE: *Women bend their knees in dancing and shake their hips which are emphasized by the bustle of the layered, wrap-around Tsonga skirt.* OPPOSITE: *A young child wearing a beaded headband.*

MARRIAGE

In traditional Tsonga society, choosing a partner was not straightforward, as the process followed a set of rules. First cousins could not marry; child betrothal was not practised, but a father might recommend girls to his son. A suitor commonly sent the woman a grass ring or thorn to indicate that he wanted to marry her. If the feeling was reciprocated, she would send him a grass ring or a thorn, confirming their relationship. After the girl's father had formally expressed his approval of the match, the boy's father sent her family a cow, which sealed the agreement. Once this stage had been reached, further negotiations would be conducted through two intermediaries representing the families.

Today working out the dowry due to the woman's family is still an important concern. Tsonga marriage is more than a relationship between individuals. It cements relationships between families, carrying privileges and obligations that transcend the death of either spouse. For example, should a wife die before producing a child, or should she be infertile, one of her relatives is supplied to bear children. When a husband dies, his relatives have to provide for his widow; if she is still fertile a younger brother might take her as a wife and produce children through her, on his deceased brother's behalf.

The traditional ceremony is still practised by many Tsonga. At the girl's departure from her home, a sacrifice is made, and she formally takes leave of her family and their ancestral spirits. This is followed by a 'handing over' of the bride to her new family. After a marriage feast at the bridegroom's *muti*, the couple are considered formally married. Traditionally the bride had to follow well-defined rules of behaviour

and etiquette in her new home. After her marriage she stayed in her mother-in-law's *muti*, helping her mother-in-law in her daily duties and in cooking the food. Her mother-in-law would instruct her in the customs of the family. She had to observe a range of rules of behaviour towards her father-in-law and his brothers. She usually moved into her own *muti* after the birth of her first child, but continued using her mother-in-law's cooking area until her husband's younger brother married. His wife then moved in with the mother-in-law.

Once a young mother moved into her own home and had her own cooking area, she, her husband and their child formed a unit in the *muti*. Initially they stayed in the husband's father's homestead, but once the husband acquired other wives the establishment of his own *muti* became necessary. The usual practice was for the son either to build next to or extend his father's *muti*. Over time this resulted in a lineage or even clan forming, as new generations added to settlements. Familial relations were strengthened through marriage, since in subsequent marriages preference was shown for the younger sisters of the first wife. A man's first wife might insist on his acquiring other wives as this enhanced her status in society and helped divide the workload of the *muti* between the wives and their children. This meant that the nuclear family developed into a functioning and economic unit, made up of different families, in which each individual had a specific status and responsibility for contributing to the common good.

RELIGION AND BELIEFS

Today over half the Tsonga belong to Christian churches, particularly the Independent Churches or the Evangelical Presbyterian Church (former Swiss Mission). Christianity is attracting increasing numbers of adherents among the educated in towns, but in rural areas traditional beliefs still have a strong hold. Traditionally many Tsonga believed in a supreme being, to whom the creation of man and the earth was attributed. The beliefs of the Tsonga lie in ancestor worship.

They believe man has a physical body *(mmiri)*, and a spiritual body with two attributes, *moya* and *ndzuti*. The *moya* (associated with the spirit) enters the body at birth, and on death is released to join the ancestors. The *ndzuti* is linked to a person's shadow and reflects human characteristics – it is that person's 'understudy' who, on death, leaves the body in the spirit world. The spirit of the dead *(swikwembu)* is imbued with the individual and human characteristics of the person. Not only is there life after death, but on entering the world of the dead the individual retains links with the living. For many Tsonga today 'society' implies an all-encompassing entity, including both the living and the dead. In order to ease the entry of the spirit of a recently deceased person into the ranks of the ancestors, a welcoming ceremony is performed shortly after the funeral. The death of a member of the *muti* causes all relatives to become ritually unclean and cleansing rituals are performed at different times of the day over a number of months.

Ancestor worship, still practised today, requires the performance of rituals, particularly during crises, under the direction of a *nanga* (diviner). The family gathers at the *gandzelo* (set aside for rituals and sacrifices) to pay homage to their ancestral spirits. Food and drink are placed in

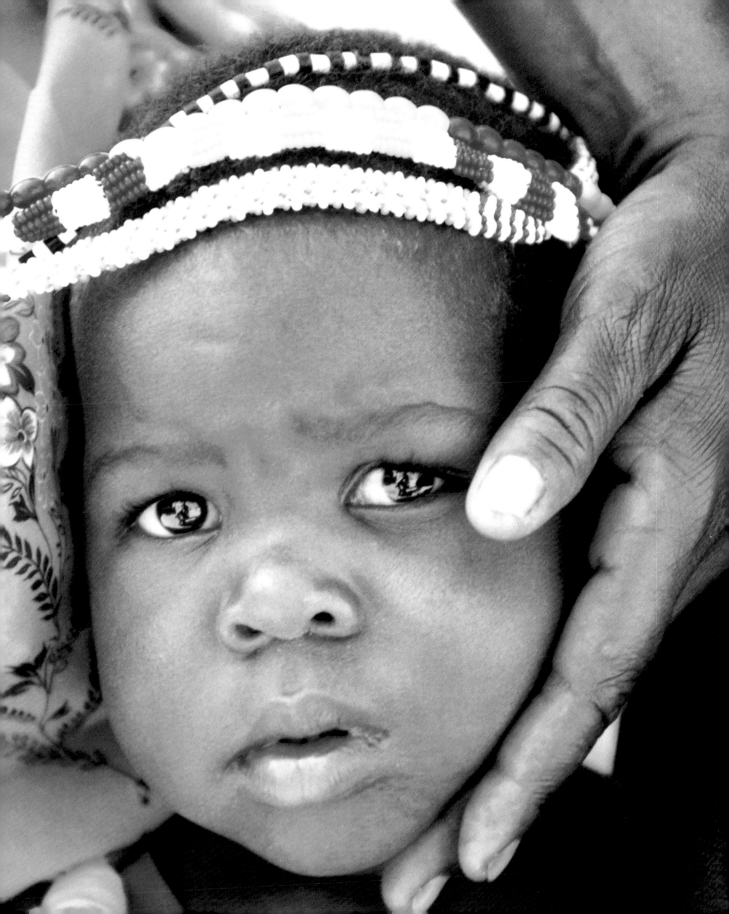

sacrifice to the ancestors who are normally thanked for providing for the people. Requests are made for their intercession with specific problems and during times of crisis. Ancestral spirits can also be approached informally and without sacrificial ceremony, through prayer.

The Tsonga also believe in good and evil spirits. Good spirits bring rain and make good happen. Evil spirits (buloyi) are manipulated by sorcerers (baloyi) who can bring great harm to the community. A sorcerer may be aware of the evil spirit within himself and use it to his advantage, but usually buloyi possess an ordinary person without his being aware of it, and leave his body at night when he is asleep.

The presence of baloyi is usually associated with persistent illness and bad luck. Occasional illness is accepted as a natural part of life, and many Tsonga believe that a sick person will heal on his own in time. Recovery can be hastened through medicinal compounds administered by knowledgeable members of the household. However, if the sickness is more serious or the cycle of bad luck persistent, it is indicative of intervention of evil spirits and a cure must be found through divination.

Divination of buloyi is done by a nanga or a mungoma, who consults with the ancestors through bones, shells and other artefacts (tinholo or mavula). The tinholo are thrown like dice onto a mat from a container; depending on the positions in which they land, the diviner determines the cause of the ailment and the course of action to rectify it.

THE TRADITIONAL ECONOMY

The Tsonga who left the coast in the 19th century brought new sources of food into the Transvaal, including cassava (manioc), certain kinds of groundnuts, potatoes and sorghum. Particularly important were the maize plants and fowls introduced by these colonists in their new areas of settlement. Most agricultural work was performed almost entirely by women, except for the initial clearing of the land which was the men's responsibility. Men also cultivated tobacco (fole). Crop harvesting was usually cooperative, done on a rotational basis, with communities in the area gathering to harvest each person's crop in turn. The owner would act as host and provide liberal quantities of beer and refreshments so that this became a festive occasion, with convivial social interaction an important feature of the event.

The Tsonga practised slash and burn agriculture. Areas of natural bush were chopped down and burnt, and crops grown on the cleared land until its fertility was drained and yields decreased. Then another piece of land was cleared and fields developed. This form of agriculture led to the steady migration of people as they had to keep moving slowly on in search of new lands. As populations increased, this often resulted in competition for land and, at times, in conflict.

For much of the 19th century elephant-hunting was an important activity on the coast and in the interior. Until the 1860s, tons of ivory were shipped through Lourenço Marques or taken to Durban annually. Hunters also sold large numbers of catskins and furs, particularly for use in Zulu and Gaza military uniforms. As elephant herds disappeared and armies demobilized, hunters killed increasing numbers of buck and sold the skins and horns to traders. Venison was an essential part of the local diet, and fishing an important communal activity. Seasonal rains turned dry river beds into roaring torrents that burst their banks,

BELOW: For over a century, Tsonga men have been working on South Africa's mines. Colloquially called 'Shangaans', they are celebrated for their dancing. Dance movements are taken to mines from isolated homesteads and return home as ethnic dances. The dancing reaches fever-pitch with vigorous drumming accompanying the participants.

THE MUSIC OF THE TSONGA

The Tsonga are well known for their rich musical heritage which is based on the playing of a wide variety of musical instruments. These can be divided into three categories: stringed, wind and percussion.

The most important stringed instruments include a notched vibrating bow *(xizambi)*, played by the musician holding the string (usually bark or twine) in his teeth, for resonance; a stick with resonators around it is rubbed up and down the notches of the bow, in time to the music. The *xitendze* is a bow with a calabash attached to it which acts as a resonator. The *mgangala*, still played today, is a hollow reed bow plucked with the fingers, while the *xipendana* is a wire-stringed bow with a thickened handle plucked with a flat piece of metal.

The wind instruments are: a cross flute *(xitiringo)* with three holes, shepherd's pipes *(nanga),* and an antelope horn trumpet *(mhalamhala)*.

Percussion instruments consist of tambourines and drums. A flat round tambourine *(tsomane)* is played by diviners to treat people possessed by evil spirits. Drums include *ndzumba* and *xigubu*, played at boys' and girls' initiation respectively, and *ngoma*, used at festive dances.

Two instruments (neither indigenous to the Tsonga) fall outside these categories: a hand piano with eight metal strips, about 10 centimetres (4 inches) long and 1 centimetre (½ inch) wide, fixed over a low saddle on a piece of wood, is played by stroking the metal strips; the other is a form of xylophone with a wooden keyboard and calabash resonators.

Tsonga music has changed since it was first recorded in the 1920s. Today it is possibly the most popular cross-over music in the country, combining local and imported traditions.

depositing large pools of water in nearby depressions. As the summer sun dried up the lakes, communities armed with conical plunge baskets swept through the shallow waters in search of fish.

At the end of the 19th century conservationists began to enclose the vast tract of land that in 1926 became the Kruger National Park. Many communities were removed from the park and those living nearby were prohibited from hunting game and fish within its borders. Hunting and fishing remain important pastimes for many of these people, but it is as poachers, rather than proud hunters, that they search for game.

For over a century, Tsonga men have found employment in South Africa's mining and manufacturing centres. Generally they have to live in hostels and pass long hours in trains and buses. Rural poverty and urban opportunity have caused well over half the Tsonga in the country to move permanently to towns. In most areas the rural economy is dependent on cash wages sent home by migrant workers in the towns. Increasingly women are also working for short spells on nearby farms.

A major problem is that there are too many people on the land. This is partly the inheritance of apartheid legislation and partly the result of an unwillingness to abandon the social ties, memories and identities associated with the land. Rainfall is relatively reliable on the slopes of the eastern Escarpment, but in many places ground and rain water are scarce. Commercial farming is undertaken in irrigable areas but the exploitation of land is held back by the old tribal allotment system and a poor transport infrastructure. For many people cattle are still a source of prestige rather than an economic value; and they are less a source of cash income than a means of acquiring wives and advertising status.

LEFT: A drummer, wearing a 'Shangaan' dancing skirt, leads musicians at a dance like the one shown on the opposite page. BELOW: Tsonga girls celebrating their initiation from girlhood to womanhood.

THE BASOTHO

The Basotho have been identified as part of a larger Sotho cohort, comprising three

broad divisions: Basotho (Southern Sotho), Pedi (Northern Sotho) (see page 124), and

Tswana (Western Sotho) (see page 116). The Basotho used to live throughout the

Highveld area but, since the mid 1800s, have been most closely associated with

Moshoeshoe's independent kingdom of Lesotho (previously Basutoland), whose

territory today is an enclave within South Africa's borders.

The first inhabitants of today's Lesotho were probably the San (*see* page 156), who left a lasting heritage in paintings on cave walls. The first Bantu-speaking people were three Nguni groups, the Phatla, Polane, and Phuthi, who crossed the Drakensberg from the east in three waves and settled in the low-lying areas south-east of the Mohokare (Caledon) River. Around the end of the 17th century, Sotho chiefdoms followed, the Peli, Phuthing, Sia and Tlokoa coming to the area from the north-west. After them came other Sotho groups, including the Koena, Fokeng and Taung.

Early in the 19th century when Shaka expanded his Zulu empire (*see* page 34), waves of social disorder swept across the once tranquil sub-continent. Sotho people in the mountains and on the western plains of present-day Lesotho (Basutoland in colonial times) and in the eastern parts of present-day Free State were also affected. Fighting became general, chiefdoms broke up, fields were destroyed, famines broke out and desperate people were reported to have resorted to cannibalism.

During this time Moshoeshoe, a Koena chief, used military strategy and political skill to defeat his enemies. He gathered a growing band of followers, both from among his defeated enemies and those fleeing the disruption, who became loyal supporters and full members of his expanding chiefdom that was the kernel of what became Lesotho. Moshoeshoe perfected the technique of withdrawing his people onto inaccessible flat-topped mountains from where they could defend themselves and wait out attacks of marauding armies that scoured the area, looking for people to plunder. He first used a mountain called Butha Buthe near the present-day town of the same name. Later he occupied a much bigger mountain, Thaba Bosiu, east of Maseru. With this as his stronghold, he moulded his men into a formidable force, beating back those who tried to invade the region. By 1831 he was undisputed ruler of the newly formed Basotho nation in an area that extended well to the west of present-day Lesotho's borders. The Rolong to the west, the Taung to the south and the Tlokoa to the east of Moshoeshoe's immediate sphere of influence remained independent allies.

Moshoeshoe was an enlightened, progressive leader who is considered as one of Africa's great statesmen. Through wisdom, patience and skilful persuasion, he created a common cultural base and political integrity for his followers. He sought to accommodate colonization by adapting Basotho social and cultural practices without destroying them. From the early 19th century traders, hunters and trekkers passed through Moshoeshoe's sphere of influence in increasing numbers. He saw that, as the numbers of colonists grew, so the potential for conflict would increase.

Realizing the need for his people to acquire Western education to compete in the new world, he sent some of his sons to school in Cape Town. He invited the Paris Evangelical Missionary Society to establish a mission station in Basutoland, and Messrs Arbousset, Casalis and Gosselin settled at Morija, near Thaba Bosiu, in June 1833. As increasing numbers of white settlers (Boers) began to establish farms in the more fertile region west of the Mohokare, pressure on land escalated. New political alliances were formed and stock raiding between Boers and Basotho became commonplace. Moshoeshoe sought the assistance of the 'great white queen of the English', Queen Victoria, petitioning for protection from the Boers. This was granted in 1848, and a British Resident Commissioner was stationed in the territory. Just six years later he was withdrawn when Basutoland was annexed to the Cape Colony. Moshoeshoe, concerned by the Boer threat, again sought British protection. In 1868 Basutoland was proclaimed British territory, and the *Basotho bahaMoshoeshoe* (King Moshoeshoe's people) became British subjects. In 1870 the aged Basotho king died, content in the knowledge that his people were 'folded in the arms of the Queen'. His lasting legacy was his unrivalled paramountcy through his unification of

Top and opposite: *Both during and after their initiation, Basotho women paint their faces and bodies with clay.*

the Basotho people in Lesotho. With the creation of a common culture, he gave the Basotho a sense of nation, and strength to stand up to their enemies. Although at times Moshoeshoe's Basotho were attacked by Zulu, Matabele, Boer and Briton, they were never defeated in battle. After his death, his sons continued to strengthen the royal house. To this day his descendants, the only heirs to the Basotho throne, are chiefs in much of Lesotho and neighbouring areas such as Matatiele in the Eastern Cape. The present monarch is King Letsie III who was crowned in 1997.

SOCIAL ORGANIZATION

At one level Moshoeshoe's Basotho were culturally and politically unified. Yet cultural divisions, based on clan- and kinship, were evident in the nation-building era and persist to today. Administrative divisions (districts, subdistricts, wards and villages), used and reinforced by the British administration of Basutoland, also persist, albeit only in Lesotho.

All Basotho belong to a clan, a social category whose members share a clan name that associates them with an animal totem or ancestor. Association is patrilineal, each person bearing the clan name of his or her father, paternal grandfather, etc. Unmarried mothers give their clan names to their child unless the father acknowledges paternity.

According to Basotho legend, people first evolved from a marsh at a mythical place called Ntsuanatsatsi. They left the marsh in groups that became clans (liboko), each of which was allocated an animal as god-protector. The totem for Moshoeshoe's clan, for example, was the crocodile (koena). Totems were sacred, endowed with the quality of a molimo (a god or invisible being), and had to be revered and feared. All members had to observe taboos and other usages in connection with the animal or object revered.

The village (motse) was the basic unit of administrative control. The number of inhabitants of a motse varied from a score to many hundreds. Most of the adult male inhabitants were related along the paternal line, but men of different clans often lived in one motse. In earlier times, dwellings were built of mud reinforced with grass, plastered over a framework of saplings. About a century ago, with the influence of missionaries, thatched houses of dressed stone became very popular. They were circular or rectangular, with one room or several. Where stones were not readily available, houses were made of mud blocks, and decorated with small stones stuck into the walls, or patterned with lines in the mud. Today many Basotho build rectangular houses with flat corrugated iron roofs. Houses built entirely of corrugated iron are found in the burgeoning towns of Lesotho and the Free State.

OPPOSITE AND THIS PAGE: *During seclusion in the lodge, initiates perform rituals, many of which train girls to be wives and mothers. Throughout Africa, masks are associated with initiation, and straw costumes and other adornments with fertility. The communal focus of initiation acts as a reminder of the maxim* motho ke motho ka batho *('a person is a person by people': humanity is defined through sociability).*

Many old Basotho villages were picturesque, blending in well with the environment. Set on raised terraces and rises, they left arable valleys and lowlands for agriculture. Efforts to aggregate settlements in the colonial 1950s and 60s forced people in Lesotho into larger villages.

As in the past, villages today consist of homesteads. Typically each has a husband and his wife and children, but many are headed by an unmarried mother, with three or four generations of children. The wide diversity in households today can be ascribed to the men's history as migrant workers on South African mines. Previously, homesteads included married sons, their wives and young children. Some men with many wives had a homestead for each wife and her children, while others just had separate dwellings within a single extended homestead.

Smaller homesteads had only one building, but some had a house, outhouses, storerooms and cooking huts. These might be connected by a reed fence or mud walls. Friends and close relatives usually lived near to each other, their dwellings contiguous or, particularly in the lowlands of Lesotho, with enclosed gardens separating them. The layout of the rural village was based on a few basic principles, which might be modified according to personal choice and the demands of the topography.

In the past, the chief's private dwelling was in the centre of the main homestead, that of his principal wife next to it, and those of junior wives in rough order of seniority around them. The court (lekhotla) was in front of his dwelling and next to it were the cattle kraal and stables.

RURAL LIFE

In earlier times daily life followed a routine, with a rigid division of labour based on age and gender. The day began at sunrise, when the family would rise. Since maize replaced sorghum as the staple food, a typical breakfast has been maize meal with boiled or sour milk and, very occasionally, meat. Household members usually ate together in the main house or, on sunny mornings, in the courtyard. When visitors were present, the men ate first and women and children ate the remains. Historically, men ate in the *lekhotla* where their wives waited on them.

The men assembled in the *lekhotla* to participate in a trial, or in helping to settle a dispute that had been brought to the chief or headman; or they discussed current issues. Those with special avocations, for instance herbalists, diviners and basket-makers, spent some time practising their professions and collecting ingredients and raw materials. Much of their time was devoted to the welfare of their livestock; when cattle-drawn ploughs were introduced from Europe the men took on the responsibility for ploughing, a task that was previously the work of women using digging sticks and hoes, although it was men who cleared new areas of bush for use as fields. On the whole, the men's routine was uncomplicated and leisurely except in times of cattle raiding. Women's duties, which varied according to season and status,

OPPOSITE: Body paint designs differ markedly, some being simple and others elaborate. This is also true of masks, which may be beaded.
ABOVE: White clay is used during seclusion, and red clay at its end.
RIGHT: Initiates carrying their possessions and firewood to the lodge where body paint is applied. PAGE 106, TOP AND BOTTOM RIGHT: Coming-out ceremonies are celebrated in a variety of ways. PAGE 106, BOTTOM LEFT: Crying with joy, this initiate is covered by her husband with a blanket. Basotho blanket patterns each have their own Sesotho name.

were more strenuous than men's. They swept and cleaned the home, prepared breakfast, fetched water, and weeded and harvested the crops. This could keep them in the fields from long before sunrise until sunset. Grinding corn was often done by older daughters. During quiet periods, women tended to the upkeep of their homes, replastering walls and floors with mud, replacing broken reeds in the fences and doing other domestic chores. What little leisure time they had was usually spent visiting friends and relatives.

From an early age children were given specific duties to perform each day. Boys herded the family's goats and, when they were older, cattle. Girls helped their mothers with domestic chores.

PAGE 107: Initiates receive gifts on their return from the initiation lodge. Their mothers wear embroidered, sometimes beaded, costumes based on designs introduced by 19th-century missionaries. THIS PAGE: Glass beads became increasingly common in the 19th century. Some reflect international fashions, as does the use of mirrors in the gifts. Small glass beads are used in older styles to decorate items like combs.

INDIVIDUAL DEVELOPMENT

Before missionaries introduced schools, education took place during initiation, marking the passage to adulthood. The missionaries objected to initiation, and it became rare during colonial years, except among the Tlokoa in the mountains. In recent years, however, it has seen a major resurgence, and most young people today are initiated.

For years before they were initiated, boys considered initiation as an important, exciting part of their upbringing, without which they could not participate in some social activities and affairs. A great deal of mystery surrounded the initiation school, which took place in a lodge (mophato) built at a secluded place in the mountains, and boys did not know what to expect. The mophato was opened by a series of rites and feasts lasting for up to three days; the initiates' parents and relatives gathered, and there was much beer drinking, and celebrations. On the third day, a black bull was killed and the initiates ate roughly roasted meat taken from its right foreleg and shoulder, cut into chunks and coated with medicines. At about midnight, they were led away to the place where the mophato would be established. At sunrise each boy was taken in turn to an isolated spot, where he was circumcised by specially trained men, who tended to all aspects of the initiation.

ABOVE: *At the coming-out ceremony female initiates show deference by looking down or covering their eyes with sunglasses.*

When the circumcision was over, the boys were left in the veld to recover. After a while, a large bowl of medicine, made from roasted butterfat mixed with a powerful narcotic made from the bulb of the *leshoma* plant, was given to them to drink, to deaden the pain. The *mophato* was built by the men responsible for the initiation process, and the initiates were inducted into it. For the next three months they were instructed in song, dance, history, and social etiquette, including behaviour and morality. Chastity, honesty, reliability, courage, humility, and respect for parents, elders and the chief were emphasized. Sexual education took the form of exhortations not to commit adultery. Physical endurance was tested through strenuous hikes across the mountains, and emotional strength by being woken at all hours to rehearse songs and answer questions. Their sleep was seldom sound, as they had only one skin blanket, and initiation was held in winter, when temperatures often fell below freezing. On the final day of the initiation, clay pots used to store food were smashed and the *mophato* was burnt down, to symbolize transition from the old to the new. The initiates were welcomed back by the chief at an elaborate ceremony.

Girls between 15 and 20 were also initiated; the process was less gruelling than the boys', but its purpose was the same: to perform a ceremony that would bring adolescent girls into the adult world. It was also a desirable, though not essential, prelude to marriage, as it was sometimes believed to encourage fertility. In some cases, when an uninitiated wife was infertile her husband would send her to be initiated.

Today initiation has a new, strong hold, tied in with a determination to use cultural activities as a mark of a Basotho identity and Africanness. While it follows similar patterns to those of the past, it has been altered to accommodate modern circumstances. A particularly recognizable change is that contemporary initiation schools are of much shorter duration than in the past, although endurance tests remain as stringent.

MARRIAGE

Arranged marriages used to be common among leaders and chief's children. Ancestry and kinship connections were important to regulate social and legal relations. The boy's father usually proposed by approaching the girl's parents. If they were receptive, he asked for a calabash of water. If her parents consented, the boy, with a few friends, formally visited the girl. If she agreed to the match, she gave him a scarf (*moqhaka*). She normally offered him food which he declined, lest it be said that 'he came for food not love'. Although the couple might not have met before, they usually approved the choice made, but in earlier times they had to go through with the marriage whether they liked it or not. More recently a greater leniency has developed – today individual choice is the norm and many unmarried women become mothers.

In the past, marriage was formalized by the transfer of *bohali* (bride wealth) from the groom's kin group to the bride's. Payments of cattle and other livestock signified that children would be of the father's clan and kin group, and not the mother's. The number of *bohali* was more or less fixed at 20 cattle, one horse, and 10 sheep or goats, but it was seldom paid in full. After a transfer of up to 10 cattle, further payments helped ally the two kin groups in bonds of reciprocity and friendship.

In the past a wedding would normally be held shortly after the marriage was arranged. Until then, the couple were not supposed to have sexual intercourse or live together. Today many marriages occur after elopement or when the man and his friends abduct *(shobela)* his chosen girl and take her to his home, where she is welcomed as if a wedding had taken place. An animal may even be slaughtered to mark the occasion, while the bride's trousseau is sent after her. The first *bohali* transfer, of six cattle or their cash equivalent, is an acknowledgement by the groom that he has had sexual relations with his wife, but does not mark his right to claim her children as members of his kin group; for this at least 10 cattle (or their cash equivalent) need to be transferred and acknowledged publicly.

Today a new couple still does not expect to have its own homestead. The bride lives with the groom's parents. She cooks, helps with chores, and works in the fields, at all times obeying rules of respect *(hlonipho)* for her father-in-law that include not saying his name or any word that sounds similar to it. In the past a man could apply for land and a building site at the start of the first season after marriage, and slowly the new household's independence in the extended family structure developed. Pressure on land today means that he may wait far longer than a year. However, many brides resist this, and demand their own households immediately upon marriage.

THIS PAGE: *At coming-out ceremonies male initiates wear beadwork made by their mothers. The garments worn include imitation leopard skin, associated with strength and virility.* ***OPPOSITE:*** *Each young man must know his ancestral praises, which he recites at his coming-out. Praise-singing has been refashioned for competitive recitation of songs and poems about the experience of work on the mines.*

OPPOSITE: Young men return home from the coming-out ceremony, laden with gifts. Like women, they look down as a sign of respect. ABOVE: Stick-fighting is common throughout southern Africa. At the lodge initiates perfect their skills, which in the past were needed by men entering the warrior phase of life; today they are more symbolic of adulthood. RIGHT: The face of another male initiate is reflected in a mirror pinned to this initiate's back, with a comb and other gifts.

RELIGION AND BELIEFS

Basotho beliefs and doctrine regarding death and the after-life have been influenced by Christian proselytizing. Consequently, incipient Basotho doctrine, beliefs and practices have been modified over time. The Basotho believe that man (motho) has two elements: the corporeal body (mele) or flesh (nama), and the incorporeal spirit (moea, also the word for wind) or shadow (seriti). The body is temporal and subject to death and decay, but the spirit is indestructible and immortal. During life the spirit lives in the body, some believe it is in the heart, others in the head, but the more general view is that it suffuses the whole body. The spirit may leave the body at night and roam about, dreams being the manifestation of these wanderings. Witches and wizards can make their spirits leave their bodies at will and direct their activities.

At death, the spirit leaves the body and hovers nearby. Until the grave is sealed, the spirit is vulnerable as it could be turned into a ghost if the dead person's tongue were cut out or a peg driven into the head by medicine men to make strong medicine. To prevent this, the body is treated with special medicines and a vigil kept over it until burial. After the final funeral rites have been completed, the spirit departs and proceeds, some believe, to the ancient home at Ntsuanatsatsi or, others believe, to a home in the sky. Spirits can be either malevolent or benevolent. It is in this spiritual benevolence that the practice of ancestor worship is grounded. Traditionally each kin group was considered to be under the direct influence and protection of its own ancestors (balimo) and the chiefdom as a whole under those of the ancestors of the chief.

Belief in ancestor influence in daily life is common, particularly in sickness. All illness used to be attributed to the ancestors, who were believed to induce sickness among the living to cause their death, thus securing companionship in the spiritual world. Today only a few maladies, e.g. hysteria, insomnia and epilepsy, are directly ascribed by some to their ancestors. They believe these can be cured by propitiating the spirits and restoring good relations, by sacrificing an animal, or by performing a neglected duty. On the other hand, Basotho continue to believe that, in general, the ancestors play an important role in curing a wide variety of diseases and ailments. Their assistance is invoked through divination by an *ngaka* (doctor), when the remedy is revealed.

An *ngaka* is very influential in local society. He or she diagnoses and prescribes remedies for ordinary ailments and diseases, alleviates and prevents misfortunes, protects against sorcery and accident and brings luck and prosperity. The *ngaka* helps in situations which people cannot control alone, or where they feel insecure. To do this, he or she uses medicines made mainly from herbs, bark, other forms of plant material and animals. The *ngaka* tends to view disease and its treatment organically, and therefore little, if any, recourse is made to the supernatural.

A *selaoli* divines ailments by throwing bones, shells etc. Depending on their position and angle, the *selaoli* diagnoses the patient's illness and interprets the treatment. The approach is generally based on the influence of supernatural phenomena and the invocation of magic. Treatment tends to rely more on ritual and appeasement of offended spirits, through sacrifices and observance of taboos, than on medicines. A *senohe* is a person who can see what others are unable to, which enables him or her to diagnose illnesses and to foretell future events.

MUSIC AND DANCE

The Basotho delight in song and dance, which accompany many ceremonies and social activities. Song is also used to mark the experiences of men's long absences as labour migrants: men compete to recite *lifela tsa litsamaea naha* (songs of the travellers) about their experiences in mine hostels and underground, and women use a similar form of recitation to lament their lives as grass widows.

The most common dances are the *mokorotlo*, the *mohobelo* and the *mokhibo*. The *mokorotlo* is performed by men for the chief on important occasions, such as political meetings, or when the chief and his followers go on a tour of inspection. It consists of rhythmic swinging backwards and forwards, combined with a regular slow foot stamping; the leader sings in a high-pitched voice which is followed by a deep throaty refrain from the group. From time to time, one of the men breaks from the group and leaps and prances before the chief, miming a battle attack. He is egged on by the others who stop singing and call him by his dancing name. He may also recite his own or the chief's praises. He then returns to his rank and the slow dancing movements continue. The *mohobelo*, performed by men, requires energy and endurance and is danced mainly in the evening, for amusement and entertainment. The *mokhibo* is a women's dance performed on the knees, the body gently rising and falling as the hands are swept upwards. An informal choir stands behind the line of dancers, singing and clapping. The *maqekha* is a special dance that forms part of the first rites of girls' initiation.

The Basotho have a variety of musical instruments. The *morupa*, a small drum used at girls' initiations, is made from a clay pot over which a taut skin is stretched, and is struck with flat hands. The *lekoko* is made of a roll of hardened cow skin which is beaten with sticks, producing a dull thumping sound. Its use is restricted almost entirely to *maqekha* seances. The *lesiba* consists of a horse-hair stretched along a stick between a quill and a holding bracket. Light sucking against the quill causes the horse-hair to vibrate, producing a haunting sound commonly accompanied by the player's voice. The *thomo* consists of a bow, across which a horse-hair or thin wire is stretched, and which is tautened with a wire fastening in the middle. The bow is attached to a calabash (or, in recent times, an old oil tin) which acts as a resonator. The instrument is played by plucking the string or picking it with a stick.

CONTEMPORARY LIFE

The strongest influence on Lesotho's Basotho is their involvement as labourers in South Africa's mining and productive industry. This represents their main source of income and has affected their practices. Its effects are obvious in their domestic arrangements (men separated for long periods from their families), and changes to how marriage is viewed (men as absentee wage-earners and women relict homemakers). Bride wealth signifies men's right to demand support from their children once they are earning, rather than just their association with a kin group.

Ancestors and diviners (*lingaka*) are implicated in men's experiences as labour migrants and women's experiences of being left at home. They are called upon to provide protection from dangers lurking in the mines and factories; they are expected to help heal injuries, physical and emotional, associated with such work; and they are turned to with the stresses faced by women left alone to care for children, fields and livestock with little, if any, money.

OPPOSITE, TOP: *Before the girls' coming-out, women of Sebokeng township (Gauteng province) dance around a fire and burn childhood belongings.* **OPPOSITE, BOTTOM:** *The blankets used by the initiates during their seclusion are discarded.* **BELOW:** *The lodge (of both male and female initiates) is burnt, attended by the woman in charge of the initiation. She ensures that nothing remains of their childhood.*

THE TSWANA

The Tswana are part of the Sotho, with three broad divisions – Basotho (Southern Sotho), Pedi (Northern Sotho), and Tswana (Western Sotho). The Tswana historically lived on the Highveld, with the Basotho. From the mid 1800s, many Sotho chiefdoms in the western Highveld began to regard themselves as part of a larger Tswana group in the colonial Bechuanaland (now Botswana). This accounts for variations in dialect, social structure and culture among the many Tswana groups that persist today.

Little is known about the early origins of the Sotho peoples of whom the Tswana now form part. According to oral tradition, they were among the Bantu-speakers who came from the vicinity of the East African Great Lakes (Victoria and Tanganyika), and made their way southwards in migrations over many centuries. Tradition also has it that they were of a common stock and later broke up into various units. Like the Basotho, their settlement patterns and places of residence were affected by the wars of the early 1800s around the time of Shaka's rise to power (*see* page 34). Unlike the Basotho, they formed into separate chiefdoms (subsequently known as tribes in colonial parlance that persists in Botswana today) rather than a single one, and located themselves in the dry west of the country, where they found San people already taking refuge from pastoralist encroachment into their hunting areas (*see* page 156).

Among the earliest to settle in the eastern, fertile parts of present-day Botswana were the Kgalagadi. When the ancestors of the Rolong and Tlhaping settled along the upper reaches of the Molopo River and gradually moved south and west, they absorbed the Kgalagadi and San in the area. Those who resisted incorporation were forced to move deep into the recesses of the Kalahari Desert where their descendants can still be found today. The area around modern-day Rustenburg, Zeerust and Lichtenburg in South Africa's North-West province was settled by Hurutshe, Kwena and Kgatla, whose settlements today reflect a strong Tswana presence. This presence is equally strong, but more dispersed and less obviously evident, throughout the cities of Gauteng province.

Evidence suggests that the ancestors of some of today's Tswana were living on the Highveld from at least the 17th century. The period from then until the early 19th century was marked by recurring political re-alignments and ruling-group fission: junior members of a chiefdom's ruling family often broke away with their followers to form a new group, which generally became known by the name of the new leader. From about 1810, however, the trend was curtailed by two factors: the turmoil created by Nguni-speaking and other invaders during the Shakan wars;

and the danger of land dispossession when white settlers came into the area, first in search of land and cattle and later in search of labour for the new diamond and gold mining industries. Both factors threatened local chiefdoms' sovereignty and led to a new trend for denser settlement in larger defensive political units than previously. With political fission having become much more difficult and unsafe, existing chiefdoms grew larger and were consolidated, often around large village-like settlements, into what are today called tribes.

SOCIAL ORGANIZATION AND TOTEMISM

Today the Tswana can be divided into very many locally autonomous (though subject to the laws of Botswana or South Africa) chiefdoms, whose size varies from a few thousand to hundreds of thousands, the larger including Botswana's eight main tribes. Each manages its affairs under a chief (*kgosi*), but there are great differences between tribes in Botswana and South Africa. The Tswana in South Africa previously fell under the Bophuthatswana Bantustan's homeland administration. Each tribe has its own territory and name, the latter usually derived from a past chief or the founder of the ruling dynasty, sometimes from the totem of the royal family, the site of a former capital, or an historical incident.

Each tribe has mixed origins, which means that members of a single tribe may differ from one another in customs and language. This is more noticeable where people incorporated into the tribe prefer to remain distinct, and use the differences as a symbol. Tswana tribes are not, and

TOP: Inventive spectacles: a new tradition in adornment that has become increasingly common. They are also sold to the tourist market.
OPPOSITE: Carved staffs with heads or figurines are quite common.

OPPOSITE: *An initiation of 2,000 men took place in Taung, North-West province, in 1997. The ceremony attests to a revival of the practice and the formation of regiments among the Tswana.* **ABOVE:** *Initiates return home wearing a variety of colourfully patterned blankets.*

have never been, closed, with fixed members. They are associations of which people may become members by birth, absorption, conquest or voluntary incorporation. Members may also be expelled by the chief, or leave voluntarily to join another tribe. Today, many Tswana in cities such as Johannesburg do not formally associate themselves with any tribe, although all recognize association with a totem (see below) and thereby acknowledge a genealogical relationship to others who share that totem.

A similar process of incorporation to that whereby tribes were formed, albeit on a much larger scale, created what is today Botswana. Its groups were brought together into one as a result of colonial intervention which created the Bechuanaland protectorate that later gained independence as Botswana. Attempts at Tswana consolidation within South Africa constituted a much more complex process related to the apartheid government's creation of the Bophuthatswana Bantustan, an entity that has been dismantled under the post-apartheid dispensation. The Tswana chiefs recognized by the apartheid system continue to claim that status and the right to rule their people.

Totemism, the veneration of an animal, plant or object, has long been an important feature of Tswana society. Each person associates with a totem, and all those associated with that totem are said to be related to one another patrilineally, normally taking the totem of their father, and father's father. People with the same totem claim that they can trace their genealogical relationship to one another.

Totemic association has long cut across tribal membership. Members of one tribe have never been associated with one totem, nor have those associated with a totem necessarily been members of one tribe. For example, the Ngwaketse have been associated with 22 different totems even though members of the chiefly dynasty share one totem.

Many myths lace Tswana folklore, accounting for how each totem came to be adopted. Codes of behaviour have been drawn up around these myths, and failure to observe them requires the perpetrator to undergo a purification ceremony to prevent illness or other misfortune.

RURAL LIFE

Tswana settlements are quite unusual in southern Africa for their large but compact size, a result, at least in part, of their arid environment. Indeed in the early mid 19th century, some Tswana settlements, which had concentrated further for defensive reasons, were more populous than Cape Town, the largest southern African colonial city of that time.

Previously it was not uncommon for all members of a tribe to be concentrated in a settlement around the chief. Some chiefs came to rule nearby settlements, through conquest of territory as well as construction of settlements for large numbers of people brought under their rule.

OPPOSITE, TOP: Participants at coming-out ceremonies include initiated men, as guardians to the initiates. OPPOSITE, BOTTOM: Although most men have worked in industry and therefore own construction helmets, others prefer to invoke the past by wearing garments made from skins of indigenous animals. ABOVE AND LEFT: The revival of initiation has led to increasing numbers of women being initiated. Modern clothing such as bras and sports shoes are combined with older forms.

The household, which has both ritual and domestic significance, is the smallest social unit, usually a man, his wife and single children, but often including married sons, and even daughters, their spouses and children. Homesteads traditionally had one or more houses and granaries in a courtyard surrounded by a reed or wooden fence, or earthen wall. A married couple often shared a house with younger children. Adolescent children of both sexes shared a house, and unmarried adults were separated by sex. The houses were used principally for sleeping and storage, cooking and social activities taking place in the open courtyard. In earlier years, members of a household built their own homestead and produced most of their food. Land, livestock, and all property were administered by the household head who allocated them to his dependants. As head of the domestic group, he expected obedience, service, and respect from his wives and children, and handled all legal dealings with outsiders. Prayer and sacrifice, performed on behalf of the household to the ancestors, were also his responsibility, though he in turn sought assistance from senior kin and clansmen in other households.

MARRIAGE

Traditionally a man's first wife was selected for him; if he could afford more than one wife, he chose others himself. Among noble groups with much property, wives to whom the man was related were preferred. Favoured were his mother's brother's daughter, father's sister's daughter, and father's brother's daughter. Marriage to this last meant that the bride wealth would stay in the byre shared by his father and father's brother.

Marriages were usually arranged by kin groups, the man's kin taking the initiative. Child betrothal used to be common, but it is no longer practised. An important part of betrothal was transfer of bride wealth *(bogadi)* from the groom's family to the bride's. A marriage was valid only when *bogadi* had been paid. This denoted the transfer of a woman's fertility (not purchase of the woman) to her husband's kin group. Only then could the children she bore become part of his kin group. If a wife failed to produce a child, her group had to replace her with one of her sisters or send an extra sister, or return the *bogadi*. The *bogadi* consisted mainly of cattle, though some Tswana (Ngwaketse and Kwena in particular) included sheep. Today, when bride wealth is transferred, combined money and cattle payment is agreed by the

groups. The number of livestock was not open to negotiation but was decided by the groom's people; the bride's family had little say in the matter other than to protest if they believed the groom's kin could afford to give more. Payment was normally due in one instalment when the bride went to live with her husband. The animals (always an even number) were assembled by the groom's father who asked his own siblings to contribute. He expected one beast from the groom's maternal uncle, since cattle received for his sister (the groom's mother) had been used to obtain his own wife. The cattle were sent to the bride's father's homestead, where they were held for a time by her father. After they had multiplied, the bride's father distributed them among his and the bride's mother's close kin, all of whom would have been asked to contribute to the bride's brother's *bogadi*. The bride's maternal uncle and eldest brother had preferential claims over cattle received as her *bogadi*.

When a man had more than one wife, each wife was entitled to her own *lapa* – houses, fields, cattle, and domestic utensils used by her and her children. However, a woman sent to replace a wife who died childless, or to bear children for a barren wife, went into the *lapa* of the wife she was replacing. On an older wife's death the resources of her *lapa*

ABOVE: *Using whatever means of transport is available, guests come from afar to celebrate the end of the young people's seclusion.*
BELOW: *The celebration extends to singing and dancing. Knobkerries are used to punctuate the movements of the dance.*

were inherited by her children. A polygynist's wives were normally ranked in order of betrothal (not marriage), a fact that left the ranking open to dispute, particularly after the husband's death. The first wife betrothed was meant to be the most senior, and her eldest son heir to the status and unallocated property of his father. Yet disputes over ranking often followed a powerful man's death as his first sons by his wives jockeyed for the right to be primary heir. When the apartheid state gave special powers to chiefs, some anthropologists found themselves caught up in such disputes, and even in court, as men vied for the right to succeed their fathers to a chieftainship and called on anthropologists to verify their claims to being first sons of senior wives.

GENDER AND AGE DISTINCTIONS

Gender and age distinctions have long been an important marker of status in Tswana society. The former was exhibited in many ways: men and women sat apart at social gatherings; and some places, e.g. the *kgotla* (council-place), were for men only. Sons were, and in some cases still are, preferred, and a woman who bore only daughters was often despised. There was a division of labour, with specific tasks allotted to people of each sex. A Tswana woman is a perpetual minor who is subject to the authority of male guardians (her father, brother or maternal uncle until marriage; her husband or his father or brother). Women were excluded from political assemblies and religious ceremonies.

Age was also the basis for distinction. As with other Bantu-speakers, the Tswana had to respect and obey those older than themselves, calling them 'father' (*rra* or *ntate*) or 'mother' (*mme*); breach of this rule was a penal offence. Respect for elders extended beyond one's kin to the whole community. Children were grouped by physical development: birth to 2 years (*masea*); 3 to 8 (*banyana*); boys (*basemane*) and girls (*basetsana*) of 9 to 13; and from 14 until they were allocated to an age-set (*magwane*, *majafela* or *maphatisi*). Boys in *maphatisi* used to wear special costumes and perform songs and dances at gatherings for their age-set, and had great freedom, especially in sexual matters. During this period, they spent much time at cattle-posts herding their father's livestock. The girls helped by fetching water, crushing and grinding maize, preparing food, sweeping the houses, and caring for younger children.

Allocation into an age-set or regiment (*mophato*) marked transition into adulthood. A *mophato* consisted of men or women of roughly the same age who were initiated at the same time. Traditionally a regiment would be created by the chief every four to seven years, when eligible boys or girls, aged 16 to 20, were initiated together. The *mophato* always included a member of the chief's family who henceforth was accepted as the leader. Many years ago the creation of a male regiment was accompanied by elaborate initiation ceremonies, known as *bogwera*. By the 1930s, however, the ceremonies had virtually disappeared, primarily because Christian missionaries regarded them as immoral and convinced 'progressive' chiefs to abandon and prohibit them. A most conspicuous feature of *bogwera* was the circumcision and seclusion of male members of the new regiment in an isolated area in the veld. During their seclusion, initiates were subjected to hardships, graded in order of precedence and taught laws, traditions and customs. Girls

ABOVE: *Donkey carts are still a traditional mode of transport in many parts of South Africa. This one has been given an unusual canopy to shield the driver from the harsh elements.*

were also initiated, in a ceremony (*bojale*) held at home. It included dancing, masquerades and some form of operation (usually branding on the inner thigh). Female initiation also included severe punishments and other hardships, and formal instruction in matters concerning domestic and agricultural life, sex and behaviour towards men.

Each *mophato* was given a name by the chief at initiation, usually reflecting a contemporary incident, such as unusual rains or drought. The *mophato* retained that name from then onwards. A person was not considered an adult and was not allowed to marry until he or she belonged to a *mophato*. Members of a regiment worked and, in the case of men, fought together, but they were also intimate companions who were equals. A sense of solidarity and regimental pride bound members: a particular sign of respect was to address a man by his regiment's name rather than his own. Members of a regiment were expected to respect all previously formed regiments and, in turn, could expect to be treated with deference by their juniors. Breaches of discipline in these and other matters associated with the regimental organization were dealt with by special *ad hoc* courts presided over by regimental leaders.

Despite efforts of Christian missionaries to end initiation early in the 20th century, there is today an ever-growing revival among the Tswana, as among others who long accepted that these teachings were not to be questioned. Initiation has become a symbol of identity in two senses: people see themselves as Tswana by virtue of having been initiated by Tswana rites; more importantly, there is a strong sense across much of the subcontinent that undergoing initiation is a mark of African identity, and that young adults who fail to undergo some kind of initiation ritual are not 'real' Africans. The practices follow patterns similar to those used in the old days, but always with new features that make them very much a contemporary phenomenon, rather than relics.

THE PEDI

Pedi was previously used to describe Sotho-speakers of Mpumalanga and Northern Province. More recently, these groups have been renamed Northern Sotho. The Pedi, as more narrowly understood, are part of the Highveld Sotho who live on the plateau around Pietersburg. Other Northern Sotho subgroups, over many of whom the Pedi once held sway, are the Lowveld Sotho along and below the Drakensberg Escarpment, and the Eastern Sotho in the Mapulaneng district, towards Lydenburg.

According to oral tradition, the Pedi can be traced back to the Maroteng, an offshoot of the Kgatla, today an important constituent of the Tswana (*see page 116*). It is believed that centuries ago, around 1500, the Maroteng were living near the source of the Vaal. Under Chief Tabane they migrated to present-day Skilpadfontein near Pretoria. Legend has it that during the reign of Tabane's grandson, Motsha, his favourite wife, Mmathobele, was accused of giving birth to a child that 'cried while still in her womb' (said to be a sign of witchcraft). The elders demanded that mother and child be put to death. To prevent this, Thobele, who had succeeded Motsha, broke away. He and a large following, including Mmathobele and her child, went east, crossing the Olifants (Lepelle) River near present-day Marble Hall. They settled on the Steelpoort (Tubatse) River in about 1650. While crossing the Leolo Mountains, they are said to have found a porcupine quill on an antheap, which was taken as a good omen. From then on the Maroteng took the porcupine (*noko*) as their totem and developed a distinctive identity. In time, the Maroteng established dominance over a broad region.

Opinion is divided on how the Pedi acquired their name. One theory is that the name is a corruption of Vhambedzi, the name of a Venda group living in the Leolo Mountains. It is believed that they taught the more numerous Maroteng interlopers their skills in iron-mongering. In the process, the Vhambedzi were steadily assimilated, the resulting amalgam coming to be known as Pedi.

By the height of their power the Pedi or Maroteng, under the leadership of Thulare (about 1790–1820), were launching frequent, successful raids on the surrounding peoples. They brought an extensive area stretching from the site of present-day Rustenburg in the east to the Lowveld in the west, and ranging south to the Vaal River (the districts that are known today as the Waterberg and Soutpansberg), under Pedi rule. The Pedi grew in numbers and strength, incorporating more and more neighbours into their realm. Under the powerful Thulare, the Pedi empire flourished and Maroteng hegemony reached its highest point.

Thulare's influence was such that he even became the spiritual leader of surrounding groups which were not under direct Pedi control. In 1824, on Thulare's death, he was succeeded by the eldest of eight sons, Malekutu, who attempted to continue expanding the Pedi sphere of influence. But his chieftainship did not last long as, legend has it, he was poisoned by one of his brothers. The Pedi were in disarray when Nguni raiders struck from the south. Historians are divided as to whether the attackers were the Matabele under the leadership of Mzilikazi, or an Ndwandwe faction under the leadership of Zwangendaba, who had broken away from Zwide after his defeat at the hands of Shaka. In either event, the Pedi were overwhelmed and all of Thulare's sons, with the exception of Sekwati, were killed. The Nguni raiders stayed for about a year, during which they harvested all the crops they could and denuded the land of cattle. Many surrounding groups became destitute and are believed, according to present-day oral sources, to have resorted to cannibalism.

Sekwati fled, with what remnants he managed to gather of the Pedi nation, across the Olifants River. For four years they sought refuge in the neighbouring, and related, chiefdom of Ramapulana. They made periodic raids against small settlements, during which they captured women and cattle. Eventually Sekwati re-crossed the Olifants River and established his headquarters at Phiring. Slowly he brought together the scattered elements of the Pedi group and re-established Maroteng dominance in the area. He managed to resist attacks from both the Swazi and Zulu, by withdrawing to the surrounding mountain fastnesses, eventually establishing his capital at Tšate, under the eastern slope of the Leolo Mountains.

TOP: *An initiate tends to a fellow-initiate's wounds after a lashing at the opening ceremony of* bodika, *the first phase of male initiation.*
OPPOSITE: *The* rabadia *(initiate guardian) dances during* bodika.

In 1845 Boer leader Hendrik Potgieter settled east of the Steelpoort, where he founded the present-day Ohrigstad. On 5 July that year Potgieter and Sekwati signed a treaty, granting Potgieter title to this land. An uneasy peace existed between the Pedi and the increasing numbers of Boers, punctuated by periodic cattle raids by the Pedi and Boer counterattacks. Pedi access to weaponry had by this time extended. The paramount chief had started to send out groups of young men to work as labour migrants in the Cape, Delagoa Bay and on the diamond fields in the northern Cape. By the 1870s, each man returning from work was paying about £1 to the paramount, which was used to buy guns and ammunition. After Sekwati's death there were disputes between two of his sons, Sekhukhune and Mampuru, about the succession to the paramountcy. This was exacerbated by the presence of the Boers, who presented a threat to continuing Pedi authority. Sekhukhune's eventual success in containing these disputes, and in establishing his legitimacy as heir, was visible in his ability to summon regiments of fighting men from the chiefdoms subordinate to his, in order to put down rebellions by other chiefs no longer content with his rule. Sekhukhune initially had friendly relations with the Boers, but intensifying struggles over land and labour saw these steadily deteriorate until finally, on 16 May 1876, the Transvaal Volksraad declared war after hearing a rumour about an impending Pedi attack on the Boer village of Lydenburg. The Boer aggressors suffered a resounding defeat.

Two months later Sir Theophilus Shepstone annexed the Transvaal Republic on behalf of the British Crown, partly spurred by Boer failure to subjugate the Pedi. After the Zulu War ended in July 1879 (see page 37), Sir Garnet Wolseley (High Commissioner for South-Eastern Africa), confident that Sekhukhune would sue for peace, offered onerous conditions, fining Sekhukhune 2,500 head of cattle. Sekhukhune refused these terms, and Sir Garnet mobilized a force of some 12,000 men, including 8,000 Swazi warriors. On 28 November 1879, after severe fighting in which over 1,000 Pedi warriors were killed, Sekhukhune was finally defeated. He was captured in a cave and imprisoned in Pretoria. And, with this, the Pedi empire was finally destroyed.

POLITICAL ORGANIZATION

The Pedi once held sway over most of the area flanked by the Limpopo, Vaal and Komati rivers, their power centralized in what is today known as Sekhukhuneland, its heartland between the Olifants and Steelpoort rivers. Although subordinate groups appeared to enjoy autonomy, social controls maintained Pedi authority. Foremost was the Pedi insistence that subordinate chiefs take their principal wives from the ruling dynasty. Over generations, this evolved into a system in which the son and heir of a subject chief was compelled to marry a cousin, and to make

OPPOSITE: *Circumcised boys prepare for the final stage of* bodika *by applying* letsoku, *a mixture of red clay and animal fat.* PAGES 128 AND 129: *Circumcised boys, in capes and holding sticks, prepare to leave the lodge and celebrate their status as* dialoga, *survivors of* bodika.

an inflated bride wealth payment to the Maroteng for this privilege. Pedi rulers and chiefs were thus tied into a relationship of inequality. In addition to bride wealth, lesser chiefs were expected to pay tribute to the paramount in other ways as well, and to keep him informed on all important events, such as the inauguration of initiation lodges. In theory, the paramount chief's court was one of appeal for subordinate peoples but, in practice, its jurisdiction tended to be restricted to political issues, such as relations between groups, boundary disputes and succession to chieftainship. Communication between the paramount chief and lesser chiefs took place by means of an elaborate system of intermediaries (batseta).

SOCIAL ORGANIZATION

Like the Sotho and Tswana, the Pedi, in pre-conquest times, lived in large villages divided into *kgoro* groups centred on family clusters favouring the paternal line. Each consisted of a group of households, built around a central area which combined meeting-place, cattle byre, graveyard and ancestral shrine. Homes were ranked in order of seniority. Each wife had her own round thatched homestead, joined to the others by a series of open-air enclosures (lapa) encircled by mud walls. In the centre was the *ngwako wa mollo* (the hut of the fire), a large enclosure containing the hearth, for cooking on rainy days. It could be distinguished from the dwellings by the *mathudi* (covered veranda) surrounding it. A circular framework of poles, about 3 metres (10 feet) in diameter, formed the perimeter wall, enclosed within a wall (leboto) made of sun-dried mud bricks. The trusses of the conical roof rested on these poles. The thatched roof extended beyond the wall of the house, creating the *mathudi*. Two smaller enclosures (ngwakana) were usually situated behind the main homestead. The homestead unit was enclosed by an angular 1.75-metre-high (5 feet 9 inches) wall made either of mud (known as the *moduthudu*), or of reeds (known as the *lefago*). This wall enclosed a wedge-shaped precinct, so that the separate homesteads, which adjoined each other and which belonged to the different wives of one man, made up a circular formation. Between the homesteads and the surrounding walls could be found the courtyards (lapa), in which Pedi people spent most of their time when they were at home. Each home had a public courtyard in front of the main hut, where guests were entertained, and a private courtyard behind the main hut, which served the members of the household.

The word *kgoro*, besides denoting this basic unit in the Pedi social structure, was used to describe the building-block of judicial and political structure as well. The unity of the disparate homesteads within the extended homestead was maintained through allegiance to a council of men, which usually met in a special open-sided thatched structure under a big tree. *Kgoro* meant both council and meeting-place. Today, many people wanting to live in a more modern style have abandoned the round style of building in favour of rectangular, flat-tin-roofed houses. Forced relocation and agricultural planning schemes instigated by the government have meant that many newer settlements, and the outskirts of many older ones, consist of houses built in grid formation, occupied by individual families unrelated to their neighbours.

ABOVE AND OPPOSITE: *Initiates celebrate on returning home from the lodge. Blending tradition with novelty, sunglasses, beaded ornaments and loincloths denote their status as survivors of the harsh rites.*

GENDER DIVISION

Pedi culture traditionally distinguished sharply between the sexes at all levels. This affected every sphere of their lives, from the knots to tie their clothes – men using reef-knots and women granny-knots – to initiation, status in the family and community, and division of labour. Women did agricultural work, and men and boys work related to cattle. Male superiority was reinforced in daily life: for example at meals men and initiated boys sat together and were served first, and women ate with the other children. Legally women were, and often still are, perpetual minors, and had to remain under a male guardian. When women married they assumed their husbands' status. Thus a woman born a commoner could become a noble on marriage and attain a

superior status to her elder sister, who then had to serve her. A woman could never rise above the level of her brother. Inheritance and succession were passed down through the male line, and women lived at their husbands' homesteads. This is, sometimes, still the case today. Many families, however, prefer to allow their daughters rather than their sons to inherit their fields and residential stands, since daughters – especially those undistracted by the obligations of marriage – are thought to be able to look after their parents better than sons can.

Traditional Pedi culture was more extreme than most other male-orientated societies in distinguishing between the sexes, tending to attribute amoral qualities and asocial behaviour to women. The inherent compulsion to do evil – witchcraft 'of the night' – was associated exclusively with women, and was passed from mother to daughter. Witchcraft 'of the day', however, was learnt, could be acquired by anyone, male or female, and was used only occasionally to harm someone.

BIRTH AND INITIATION

The birth of the first Pedi child was an event of great importance: it not only brought a new member into the household, but also raised the mother to the highest status attainable. In addition, it concluded the obligations of the mother's family to the father and his family, while proving the manhood of the father and perpetuating his line. Confinement and the birth of the first child normally occurred at the home of the mother's family. After the birth, both mother and child returned to the father's household where a feast was held, to which the mother's family made a contribution of meat and beer. This discharged their final obligation to the father's family to provide a child through one of their members, for which *magadi*, a set number of cattle and livestock or their monetary equivalent, was paid. In recognition of the mother's new status, the father built a separate dwelling for her, as she now had the right to possess and control her own homestead. On her return with the baby, mother and child were secluded for a period in the new homestead. After this, a special feast (*ngwana o tswa ntlong*) was held to celebrate the arrival of the child in the paternal home. During the feast, ceremonies were performed which concluded the initiation of the child into the family and the mother into her new status.

In traditional Pedi society, gender distinction was a fundamental characteristic of initiation, emphasizing the essential differences between the sexes. Initiation simultaneously marked the passage to adulthood and invested the initiate with citizenship of the community, and, in the case of males, the right to participate in political and jural functions. An important benefit that initiation traditionally gave was to reinforce Pedi paramountcy over the other peoples within their empire or sphere of influence: lesser chiefs had to obtain permission from the Pedi paramount chief before they could start a new initiation. The right to grant or refuse permission enhanced the authority of the Pedi paramount chief, in that it gave him control over the right to citizenship and political and jural participation. In more recent times, with individual chiefs at liberty to license initiation independently of central control, the ceremony is a source of considerable wealth to these chiefs, who are often accused of misusing the funds they collect in this way.

Initiation, known either as *koma* (from *go koma*, to circumcise) or *lebollo* (from *go bolla*, to hurt), was one of the most sacred institutions and important cornerstones of traditional Pedi culture. Attendance at the initiation schools was compulsory for all boys and girls of the appropriate age (which varies widely), but the two sexes were initiated separately. The boys underwent two sessions; the girls one. Through initiation they attained full adulthood and were incorporated into a distinct group. Initiation is still important to many Pedi, but has become a source – or perhaps a reflection – of social division. A major cleavage in contemporary Pedi society, between *baditshaba* (traditionalists) and *bakriste* (Christians), derives partly from contrasting religious beliefs but also from attendance or non-attendance at initiation. It may also reflect differences of social status and education. Early converts to mission Christianity were required to transfer their allegiance from the chief to the missionary, and their passage to adulthood was marked by being confirmed rather than initiated. The split between the two categories of people has occasionally flared up, in the contemporary period, with traditionalist youths kidnapping Christian ones and forcing them to become initiated against their will. While much of the Pedi initiation has remained the same, there may have been certain changes since the details were gathered on which the following account was based. It is therefore rendered in the past tense.

The first of the boys' sessions (*bodika*) introduced them into full membership of the group. The second (*bogwera*) incorporated them into the society of men, according to the class and position in society to which they were born. *Bogwera* entitled the man to sit around the ceremonial fire and take part in political and judicial activities. In contrast, the girls' initiation (*byale*) simply incorporated them into membership of the group. They were barred from participating in any political and judicial activities. They were also excluded from the elite status which males attained through their second initiation session.

The timing of initiation, which was (and is) always in midwinter, was dependent on the presence of a high-ranking son or grandson of a chief among the initiates. He was leader of the initiation lodge and life-long leader of that regiment or age-set (*mphato*); in this way the men were linked to the chieftainship. A few days before the *bodika*, a master (*rabadia*) and a deputy-master (*moditiana*) were nominated by the chief's inner council to control and direct the ceremony. They carried out their functions as the envoy of the chief. A medicine man (*thipana*) was also elected to perform the circumcision of each initiate. He was to be from outside the group, to reduce the threat of witchcraft.

During the night of the opening ceremony, the *badikana* (initiates of the first session) lined up in single file, with the leader in front. Behind him, in descending order of rank, were the others from the royal *kgoro*,

followed by the boys from the next *kgoro*, down to the boy from the most inferior *kgoro*. The boys bent over and were given, in descending order, two severe lashings on their naked backs by the *rabadia*. The lashing by rank consolidated for ever the tradition that status was conferred by birth alone, and not by personal prowess. This process underscored the function of initiation in Pedi society, both to educate, and also to position candidates within the structure of the group.

Before dawn the next day, the war-horn *(phalafala)* was blown and, on the order of the *rabadia*, the *badikana* went to a river, where they were circumcised by rank. After the operation the boys sat in the cold water of the river, which helped to numb the pain. After resting for the day the boys were marched to the *mphato* (initiation lodge), again in rank. The lodge was constructed out of wooden poles and laths lashed together in a lattice work, which was then covered with grass and branches. It had two entrances, one in the east, for the exclusive use of the men officiating at the initiation school, and the other in the west for the boys. The men and boys also slept separately. Each *kgoro* had its own fireplace, around which the initiates of that family gathered and slept. The fires built had great symbolic significance, as they were lit by an ember taken from the chief's fire and, for the duration of the *bodika* initiation process, they were not allowed to die.

Daily routine during the whole *bodika* session varied very little. Most of the day was taken up by hunting and practising the crafts of men, such as leather and woodwork. The early mornings and late afternoons were devoted to formal instruction and the singing of initiation songs. The *badikana* were taught the masculine qualities of courage and endurance, obedience to their fathers, with a great deal of stress on demonstrating deference towards and respect for the chief. Traditional lore and formulae (which included history, rituals and rules) were taught using archaic language which had to be learnt by rote. Throughout, the boys were subject to tests of endurance, including daily lashings. Discipline was rigidly enforced, and death during initiation was not unknown.

The members of the *bodika* consisted of an age-set which, shortly before the end of the *bodika*, received a name. This group used to have a military function and was under the command of the *kgosana ya mphato*. The members measured their age by referring to this regimental name, distinguishing themselves in age from the members of other initiated regiments. Once the naming process was finalized, the group was notified of the date the *bodika* would end, and food was prepared for a great feast to celebrate the homecoming of the initiates.

On the final morning, the initiates washed off the white colouring with which they were decorated throughout the process. Each father cut his son's hair and gave him a new loincloth in recognition of his newly acquired manhood. The boys' bodies were then smeared with a mixture of fat and red ochre. At this stage they were known as *dialoga* (survivors). They were lined up in rank order and ceremonially lashed for the last time. After this, they marched off without looking back while the *rabadia* set fire to their *mphato*.

Some two years later the *bogwera* initiation session was convened. In form, this was almost identical to the *bodika*, except it was less formal and lasted for only about a month. During this session, the initiates were incorporated into male society, which enabled them to fulfil the

OPPOSITE: *Girls in beaded ornaments and with vanity cases celebrate at the end of initiation.* **ABOVE:** *A girl undergoing initiation wears the short stringed front-apron (*lebole *or* theto*) and short leather back-apron (*nthepana*). Her mother wears the ceremonial dress of a married woman. She has a long smocked shirt (*hempe *or* nyebelese*), a leather front-apron (*lebole*) and the long leather back-apron (*nthepa*). A headscarf (*šeše*) has replaced the mud and graphite hairstyle (*mokamo*) which was formerly associated with married women.*

responsibilities of men. The *bogwera* would also cement the bonds of brotherhood created through membership of regiments. Lifelong ties of solidarity and cooperation were created during the *bogwera*. Since the onset of labour migration, these ties have formed the basis of groups of 'home-boys' – *banna ba gagešu* – who have helped each other find accommodation and work in town, repatriated the bodies of deceased members, and kept each other informed about matters of importance which occurred in the countryside while they were working in town. Such groups even formed the core of fledgling ANC branches in the countryside and were at the heart of the 1958 Sekhukhune revolt, in which the Pedi rebelled against state attempts to control the use of land and cattle and to interfere with the chieftaincy.

The stages of male growth and development in traditional society were clearly defined and required the fulfilment of set rites of passage. These stages can be summarized as: baby (lesea); boy (mošemane); youth (lešoboro); circumcised youth (modikana); member of a short transitional period (sealoga); initiate (leagola); initiate undergoing the bogwera (legwere); and finally adult man (monna).

On the day the bogwera initiation session ended, the byale (the girls' initiation) began. Only girls who had undergone a puberty ceremony were eligible to be initiated. Assisted by the old women, the byale was directed by the principal wife of the chief. Although the chief had the overall responsibility and authority for the byale, he was not directly involved in it in any way.

The girls were summoned to the chief's kgoro by the blowing of the war-horn (phalafala). They were led to a secluded place in the veld where all their hair was cut off. Their mothers gave them a special leather apron (kgakgo) which they wore in front, combined with a back-apron (nthepana). They also wore a short smocked shirt (gentswana or nyebelese). The smocked style was originally introduced by missionaries but has become an article of clothing which denotes a traditionalist orientation. Their bodies were smeared with a mixture of red ochre and fat, after which they had to collect firewood and return to the chief's kgoro for the night. Before sunrise they were lined up in rank and treated with protective medicines. This was followed by individual lashings in rank order, prior to being marched off into the veld. At a secluded spot they underwent a frightening circumcision charade which emulates that undergone by boys. The girls would then be taken to a lodge where they were secluded for a month. During this time they received formal instruction on the work and duties of women. They

LEFT: A woman cooking porridge (pap). Her ceremonial garb is described as 'Sotho', a term which emphasizes the traditional nature of her clothing. Parties are one of the few occasions – apart from rituals such as initiation – when women wear Sotho dress.
BOTTOM LEFT AND BELOW: At the party, women dance and sing kiba. In country areas, this style of music is also called lebowa – like the name of the 'homeland' which was set aside for Pedi and other Northern Sotho. The dancers wear a more modern form of the traditional married women's smock (hempe or nyebelese) – it uses much less fabric than the one on page 133.

were taught to respect all men, particularly the chief, given instruction in sexual matters and subjected to endurance tests. Singing and dancing played an important part in the *byale* and a special drum (*moropa*), which was normally kept by the chief, was used for this purpose.

After the seclusion, the girls bathed and participated in rituals and were then allowed to return home. In traditional times their legs were tied together at the knees and the girls' bodies were covered from the neck to the ankles in grass mats. They had to remain in this stage of transition for nine months, or until the harvest had been reaped. In recent times this period has been considerably shortened, to accommodate the demands of formal schooling. During this time the initiates assisted their mothers by day in their chores and retired at night to a special enclosure *(thupantlo)* which was built behind the homesteads of every *kgoro*. Here their tuition continued in the form of special initiation songs and monotonous repetition of formulae.

At the conclusion of the *byale*, the initiates were secluded in the veld for about 10 days while *dikomana* (initiation secrets) were revealed to them. The initiates were incorporated into a regiment, whose leader was the senior initiate. Again their hair was shorn and they bathed, after which they were smeared with fat and ochre. They proceeded to the royal *kgoro*, where they remained for two days. During this time the initiate was known as a *sealoga*. Once this period was over, they

TOP LEFT: *A woman in* šеšе *headscarf serves sorghum beer.* **TOP RIGHT:** *Women play the* kiba *drums* (meropa) *with lengths of rubber hosepipe. Complex polyrhythms accompany the dancing; skilled dancers match their steps to the rhythms.* **ABOVE RIGHT:** *A decorated courtyard* (lapa) *lying between and linking the various buildings* (ngwako) *of the homestead. It was in these enclosed areas that many of the transactions of Pedi life occurred.* **ABOVE LEFT:** *A woman, balancing a large clay beer pot on her head, walks past her courtyard* (lapa).

bathed in the river for the last time. Their parents gave them new clothes, which consisted of the stringed apron of the unmarried girl in the front and, reaching to the ankles, the back apron of married women (*nthepa*). They wore a longer version of the smocked shirt (*hempe* or *nyebelese*). They changed their hairstyle to the *tlopo*, where the hair was formed into a flat bun on top of the head with the back and side hair shorn off. This was once the everyday head-dress of marriageable and married women, but its use is now restricted to initiation itself. The initiated girl was now known as *mothepa*, a stage leading up to full initiation (*kgarebe*). After this the girl was eligible to marry.

Pedi girls passed through stages of development and incorporation into society: *lesea* (baby); *mosetsana* (girl); *lethumaša* (uninitiated girl); *kgarebe* (mature maiden); *sealoga* (member of a brief period of transition); *mothepa* (initiated maiden); *kgarebe* (maiden with recognition of her status of maturity). However, a female attained the status of being a woman (*mosadi*) only once she was married and had borne a child.

MARRIAGE

Like other Bantu-speaking peoples, a Pedi marriage (*lenyalo*) does not just legalize a relationship between individuals: it is a group concern, legalizing a relationship between families. In essence, it involves the transfer of payments (*magadi*) from the groom's relatives to the bride's relatives. In return, the bride's family publicly transfers the fertility capacity of the bride to the place of the groom (*bogadi*), and thus their commitment to the groom and his relatives is fulfilled only after the birth of a child. Marriage was virtually obligatory in traditional Pedi society. It was a legal process and did not involve religious rites. Unlike the rites of passage involved in the initiation process, marriage did not change the status of either the bride or groom, but instead it advanced their existing status as fully initiated adults in Pedi society. The new status acquired through marriage was a legal one, which increased the powers, obligations and duties of a status already acquired.

ARTS AND CRAFTS

Important Pedi crafts include pottery, house-painting, woodworking (especially making drums), metal smithing and beadwork. Traditional music (*mmino wa setšo*) has a six-note scale, formerly played on a plucked reed instrument (*dipela*). Today musicians use instruments such as the Jew's harp and the German autoharp (*harepa*), which have come to be regarded as typically Pedi. Perhaps best known is the *kiba* dance, which used to be rural but is now a migrant style. The men's version has an ensemble of players, each with an aluminium end-blown pipe of a different pitch (*naka*), producing a descending melody with rich harmonies. Men wear kilts (harking back to Pedi involvement with the Allies in World War II) with traditional regalia. The women's version features songs (*dikoša*) in which individuals improvise on older lyrics. Singing and dancing *kiba* is one of the few occasions when women wear the smocked clothes of the *kgarebe*, first worn after initiation. Both men and women's *kiba* are accompanied by an ensemble of drums (*meropa*), now made of oil-drums and milk-urns.

RECENT DEVELOPMENTS

Subsequent to their defeat at the hands of the British, the Pedi were relegated to a series of officially designated reserves. Foremost among these was the Pedi heartland, Sekhukhuneland. Together with the adjoining reserves, Sekhukhuneland was incorporated into Lebowa in the 1960s, designated as a homeland for the Northern Sotho people.

Population increase and land degradation in these reserve areas have made it increasingly difficult to live from cultivation alone. Men have been compelled to leave home and work for wages. But there is still a keen commitment to the maintenance of fields, with ploughing done during periods of leave or, increasingly, by professional ploughmen. The typical pattern has been for Pedi men to spend a short time working on nearby farms, and later to find a job on the mines or in domestic service, and then in industry. The management and execution of all other agricultural tasks have been entrusted to these men's wives.

Although subjected to spiralling controls in their lives as wage-labourers, Pedi men fiercely resisted all direct attempts to interfere with the 'home' economy – the sphere of cattle-keeping and agriculture. Families have continued to practise cultivation and to keep cattle, not so much to subsist but more as a way of showing their long-term commitment to the rural social system in order to gain security in retirement. More recently, women have begun to work for wages as well. Some work only before marrying, for short periods on farms. Others, divorcing or remaining unmarried, have since the 1960s been working in domestic service in the towns of Gauteng.

Despite their military defeat during the 19th century, the Pedi have continued to hold the chieftainship in high esteem. Especially in Sekhukhuneland, in which the former seat of the paramountcy Mohlaletse is situated, the Pedi have made concerted efforts to reconstruct the chiefship. These exertions became most strenuous during the 1950s, when the apartheid government was attempting to use local chiefs as go-betweens in their 'Bantu Authorities' system of rule. Pedi resistance against Bantu authorities in the 1958 Sekhukhune revolt resulted in the deportation of Morwamotše, Sekhukhune's grandson and heir. Migrants played a key role in carrying political ideas and organization strategies between town and countryside, and a number of ANC branches were founded during this era.

Although a number of Pedi have settled permanently in the towns of Gauteng, most continue to have an abiding commitment to Bopedi (the place of the Pedi) in the countryside. Chiefs and commoners have witnessed the dismantling of the apartheid government's Lebowa and its subsuming within the new South Africa's Northern Province.

OPPOSITE LEFT, TOP: Kiba or lebowa dance leader, wearing beads, smock and šeše headscarf. The whistle around her neck is to call the dancers to order. OPPOSITE RIGHT, TOP: A woman grinding corn with a grindstone. She is demonstrating a skill of her girlhood, but few women grind their own corn or sorghum nowadays: most purchase meal ready-ground. OPPOSITE RIGHT, MIDDLE: A woman using paint to decorate the walls of the lapa. House-painting, made so famous by the Ndebele (see page 64), was originally learnt by them from the Pedi. OPPOSITE LEFT, BOTTOM: A woman in a traditional smock inspects the results of her wall-painting handiwork in the lapa. OPPOSITE RIGHT, BOTTOM: A kiba dancer plays the part of a policeman in a dramatic parody of (white) male authority. Kiba policemen arrest male party-goers during the dance, handcuff them, and fine them on various pretexts – like failing to dress up in jacket and tie for the occasion.

THE NTWANA

Kwarrielaagte in Mpumalanga province is the chief village of the Ntwana. Purchased

from a white farmer at the beginning of this century, Kwarrielaagte's architectural

configuration, like the traditions, modes of dress and artistic practices of its

inhabitants, reflects a stable social hierarchy. Each member of the group has a strictly

assigned status and position, according to both nature and social custom within a

frozen landscape, unsullied by shifts in historical, social and cultural tides.

Although classified as Northern Sotho, the Ntwana are believed to be of Tswana (Western Sotho) origin. They can be traced to the Bakwena-Bamangwato and were probably related to the Rolong. Until they purchased Kwarrielaagte in 1903, the Ntwana were constantly migrating from area to area, mixing with other groups. It was only when the Ndebele chief Mzilikazi (*see* page 64) attacked groups in the then Transvaal in the 19th century that the Ntwana, searching for protection, became influenced by Northern Sotho groups, particularly the Pedi.

The cultural exchanges between the Ntwana and Pedi are evident in similarities in dress (women from both groups wear the missionary-introduced smock as part of their traditional dress), custom, ritual, architectural configuration (both groups live in traditional Northern Sotho settlements) and language. The Ndebele are also known to have shared close ties with the Ntwana, reinforced through intermarriage, mutual participation in initiation rituals and similarities in female adornment, such as the beaded neckbands worn by women from both groups. All three groups observe a strict division of gender roles and depend on the rural agrarian economy for their survival. Like the Transvaal Ndebele and Pedi, by the end of the 19th century the Ntwana were faced with colonial subjugation and the migrant labour system which served to shatter the rural economy. These historical circumstances augmented the emphasis on stable values and traditions in order to preserve a way of life that was being transformed.

The name Ntwana ('hard-headed' or 'warrior') possibly derives from a legend surrounding the break-away of a splinter group from the Bamangwato. Apparently, one of the chief's sons broke a taboo concerning the consumption of bull flesh. He was consequently excommunicated and departed with a band of renegades in the late 1780s to form the Ntwana group. Today the group mostly inhabit the Moutse area, south of Groblersdal in Mpumalanga province. Although the Ntwana form the majority of the inhabitants of Moutse, the area is also populated by Pedi, Swazi, Sotho and Ndebele communities.

Until 1986 the different communities co-existed peacefully, largely sharing value systems, engaging in mutual cultural exchanges and even inter-marriage. This harmony was shattered in 1986 by the forced incorporation of Moutse into the former homeland of KwaNdebele. The Ntwana resisted resettlement; as the once politically conservative community became more militant, the area around Dennilton and Kwarrielaagte became a battleground, not only between pro- and anti-government forces, but between neighbours and families as well. Yet, in the midst of the turmoil, many Ntwana traditions continued, particularly among the women. In the absence of their menfolk – most of whom worked as migrant labourers – they were forced to maintain both the rural economy while continuing their traditional roles as wives and child-bearers.

RITES OF PASSAGE

The role of Ntwana women as wives and mothers is reflected in changes in the traditional dress worn at different stages of development. The phases are: *lesea* (baby); *mosetsana* (girl); *lethumaša* (uninitiated girl); *sealogana* (transitional period); *mothepa* (initiated girl); and *kgarebe* (mature teenager). Only after marriage and particularly after the birth of her first child is an Ntwana woman accorded the status of *mosadi* which means both woman and wife.

Rites of passage, such as coming-out rituals, weddings and burials, are performed in the yards of homesteads. Before the initiation ceremonies (*byale*) which form part of the *koma* (the entire initiation period), adolescent girls undergo a puberty rite. This is a private ceremony, as

TOP: *An Ntwana woman with her hair in the bicycle seat (tlhotshwana) style.* **OPPOSITE:** *Female initiation includes ritual hair cutting.*

OPPOSITE: *Before initiation ceremonies* (byale) *are performed, girls undergo a puberty rite, but they are accorded official group status only after initiation.* **THIS PAGE:** *The ubiquitous* sehlora *(squirrel's tail) comprises beaded concentric circles, usually white on the outside, black or blue in the inner circles and red and white in the centre.*

Ntwana girls are accorded official group status only after initiation. During initiation, like male initiates, they are in a state of transition – neither children nor adults. During this period, when they are vulnerable to destructive forces, they are kept in seclusion.

When a young girl begins to menstruate she is secluded for several days. She is then given a leather foreskirt (lebole) sparsely decorated with rows of buttons and swaying leather tassels, signifying a new phase in her evolution from child to woman. She also wears an ntepana, a smaller version of a married woman's rear apron. Like the foreskirt, it is usually adorned only with buttons and loose swinging vertical strings of beads similar to those found on the rear aprons of married women.

The byale is directed by the chief's principal wife, older women and initiated girls. The process includes ritual hair cutting, in which the girls' hair is shaped like a bicycle seat (tlhotshwana) and rubbed with charcoal and fat, while their faces are made up with fat and red ochre. The girls are given leather aprons by their mothers which they wear with an ntepana. Their breasts are uncovered, their arms laden with grass bangles (ditokwa) and they wear beads (mathala) around their necks.

After their initial breaking-in period the initiates spend a month in a lodge (mphato) where they receive sexual and domestic instruction. They undergo a simulated circumcision and the stretching of the labia minora. This stage is characterized by nocturnal singing and dancing, reinforcing the bonds between the initiates. They are taught how to make fertility dolls (gimwane or popenyane) and mats from river grass (legolo) and to decorate domestic calabashes (mogope). At the final stage of their initiation, the girls are called boramaswaile, and are covered with ash before returning home where they are accorded the status of kgarebe.

For Ntwana boys, the initiation process – like that endured by their female counterparts – underscores their transitional status and also prepares them for their future role in society. Newly circumcised males are dressed in female gear and their hair is styled in the bicycle seat design of female initiates. Round their waists they wear beaded grass hoops arranged in the order of white, red and black or blue, followed by pink – approximating the colour arrangements worn by both initiated and married women. After initiation, Ntwana men shed all signs of androgyny and assume strictly demarcated, defined social roles.

MARRIAGE

Marriage among the Ntwana is not an individual affair but a group concern, legalizing the relationship between relatives. It also confers adult status on the bride and groom. Although there are no kinship taboos among the Ntwana, cross-cousin marriages are still favoured. The wedding (lenyalo) takes place over two days, first at the home of the bride's parents and thereafter at the groom's family homestead. Despite the fact that many Ntwana are Christians, marriages are conducted according to Ntwana custom. The groom dresses in a city suit

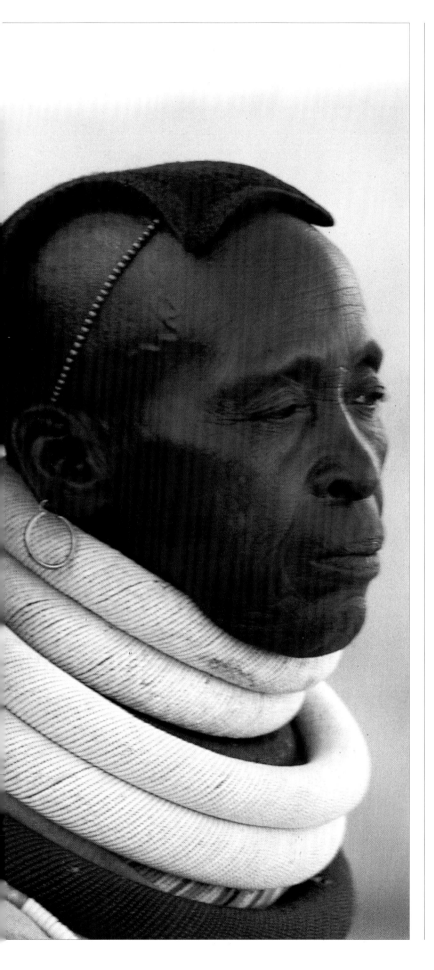

adorned with a bib made from animal hide. By contrast, the bride dons full traditional bridal regalia, which includes a feather atop her head or a beaded headband, usually in red, blue or white. In addition to a frontal and rear apron, she also wears a blanket which she must keep around her shoulders on entering her mother-in-law's household. This suggests that the Ntwana bride is made to feel conscious of her foreigner status until her mother-in-law performs a ritual which signifies that the newest addition to the family is indeed welcome. But, while in theory the Ntwana bride shares her husband's status, in actuality she is only regarded as an adult on the birth of her first child, once her fertility has been proven. It is only then that she may wear the traditional paraphernalia of Ntwana women – decorated frontal and rear aprons – on a daily basis.

THE ROLE OF WOMEN

Women in particular epitomize and reflect the unchanging ethos of the Ntwana. Their modes of dress, the objects they produce and the rites they perform reinforce their role as the upholders of tradition and sustainers of the rural economy in the face of urbanization and in the absence of their menfolk, most of whom have been absorbed into the migrant labour system. As closer examination of this virtually unrecorded group reveals, their identity as a distinct cultural group is inextricably bonded to both the distant and recent history of South Africa.

Although the shape of the frontal apron (thetho) worn by both Ntwana and Pedi women is identical, it differs in terms of decoration. Unlike Pedi pelts, which are incised with cross-hatched patterns, the surface of Ntwana aprons is usually smooth except for the presence of standardized decorative motifs. Produced from goatskin or occasionally oxhide, the frontal and rear aprons symbolize the most significant stage of the Ntwana woman's life: her marital status and consequently her acceptance as an adult woman in the community.

The frontal apron is sparsely decorated; their most commonly recurring adornment is the sehlora ('squirrel's tail'): a rosette-like motif with concentric circles usually decorated with white beads on the outside, black or blue on the inner circles, and red and white in the centre. The sehlora appears to have great significance to the Ntwana as it recurs on most of their traditional regalia, and is worn on the head.

The rear apron (ntepa) worn by Ntwana women is shaped into an inverted V formed by a triangular gap framed by two tapering leather flaps (lekobe). Among the Pedi, this form has been interpreted as representing female genitalia but Ntwana scholars believe it represents the hind legs of a goat. Both suggest associations with female fertility. The

LEFT: *The bicycle seat hairstyle of these women is also adopted by male initiates, whose androgynous dress underscores their transitional status.*
PAGES 144 AND 145: *An Ntwana woman is only regarded as an adult after the birth of her first child, i.e once her fertility has been proved. Only then may she wear on a daily basis the traditional gear of Ntwana women – smocks, beaded neckbands and decorated aprons.*

emphasis on Ntwana women's central role as childbearers finds its most visible form in the *gimwane* or *popenyane* – a traditional fertility doll constructed from plaited sisal, wool and beads. The skills to produce these dolls are passed down from mother to daughter. Little girls pretend the dolls are the progeny of their boyfriends, who are invited to participate in a dance competition, the outcome of which determines the leader of the prepubescent group. The young boys usually congregate at the home of one of the girls, who places each *gimwane* in a line. The 'fathers' and 'mothers' form two rows on either side of the dolls and dance with their partners. The winner, as judged by a parent, receives a goatskin as a trophy. Often the other boys subsequently stage a fighting contest to confirm the real leader among them.

The coloured beaded waistbands around the lower half of the *gimwane* are usually arranged in a traditional uniform colour pattern: two white bands on top, followed by one red, one blue, one pink and sometimes one white band at the bottom. This colour arrangement approximates that worn by initiated and married Ntwana women around their waists. White, red and blue or black are common colours among the Ntwana because of their associations with soil-types (such as ochre for red), which are believed to possess magical, healing powers.

Although the fertility dolls have no specific sexual articulation, the gender of some *gimwane* may be determined by the shapes of their frontal and rear aprons. Male *gimwane* tend to have rectangular loincloths while the female dolls may be identified by the V-shaped aprons which resemble the *ntepana* (rear aprons) worn by uninitiated Ntwana girls. Such traditional features are becoming increasingly rare on the *gimwane* dolls, in contrast to the profusion of ornamentation found on the more recently produced dolls. This is due largely to the fact that the *gimwane* is no longer invested with cultural symbolism. It has become increasingly commodified, and adapted or modified to suit the desire for decorativeness on the part of its mainly white market.

THE HOMESTEAD

The dwellings at Kwarrielaagte reflect the overall sense of community and solidarity among the Ntwana. Their homesteads are microcosms of the larger community and represent the private world of the family within the broader society. Access from the communal courtyard (*kgoro*) to the homesteads is via public passageways, radiating at every two or three alternate homesteads. Ntwana women are entitled to their own homesteads after the birth of their first child. In cases where a man has more than one wife (the Ntwana are polygynous), two or three more homesteads are built adjacent to one another. Ntwana women decorate the outer and inner main walls of the courtyards framing the homestead. Packed and plastered by the women, the walls are comprised of earth, dung and coarse aggregate stone. They are decorated at the end of the harvest, at the beginning of the dry season and during the period between the harvesting of the crops and the sowing of the next year's produce. Mural decoration is one of the first tasks undertaken by a new bride, but it is not necessarily a solitary task as female relatives often lend a hand. Red, white and black coloured soil is combined (*limo*), which is used both to decorate the walls and

OPPOSITE: Female initiates wear leather aprons and rearskirts. Their arms are decorated with grass bangles and their necks and heads with beads. ABOVE: Male initiates wear beaded grass hoops around their waists. PAGES 148 AND 149: An Ntwana wedding (lenyalo) occurs over two days, at the homes of the bride's and the groom's parents. The groom wears a Western suit with an animal hide bib, but the bride dons full traditional bridal regalia. She wears a blanket which she must keep around her shoulders on entering her mother-in-law's house.

serve as a protection against witchcraft. Once these pigments have been combined, the women paint the walls with it using either their fingers or sticks. Unlike colourful Ndebele murals with their spectacular designs, Ntwana mural decoration is sparse, minimalist and monochromatic, consisting of delicate geometric patterns or criss-cross motifs. While the object is to beautify the homestead, the soil types are also believed to be imbued with medicinal, protective or healing functions.

The same colour triad (red, white and blue/black) recurs in all aspects of Ntwana material culture, and various elements which are either associated conceptually or visually with the colour triad are used extensively in both rituals and everyday situations. However, the triad pervades beyond the context of rites of passage and formal social rituals. It appears on Ntwana female apparel, in the beadwork of the frontal and rear aprons, and on the rosettes worn on the side of Ntwana women's heads. Furthermore, its soil constituents are used on Ntwana homestead walls as a magical, religious means of protection against both natural and mystical causes of misfortune.

TRADITIONAL BELIEFS

For the Ntwana, rain is not merely the physical source of regeneration. It is also the symbol of spiritual fertility and a sign that nature and society are in harmony. In order to ensure the smooth continuation of the cosmic order, rain-making rites are held annually. Before this event the rain is invoked through the symbol of the lightning bird (tladi). Widely believed to be a Cape fish eagle, this bird is distinguishable by its red, white and black feathers. It is believed that the lightning bird is trapped within an object called the lehadima, an ox horn decorated to resemble a bird with red, white and black concentric circles. The lehadima is used extensively by male and female diviners (ngaka or mapale) to invoke the rain which will ensure the fertile regeneration of both the land and the community.

The Ntwana have contradictory attitudes towards symbols of fertility. For example, the colour red is regarded both as a sign of fecundity and danger. Lightning is regarded as the harbinger of rain, yet the Ntwana also believe it may be trapped by witches and misdirected in order to subvert the natural fertile order of life. Likewise, women, who are responsible for the overall fecundity of both land and womb, are also

RIGHT: When a young girl begins to menstruate, she is placed in a secluded place for several days. Thereafter she is given new clothes – a short leather foreskirt (lebole) sparsely decorated with rows of buttons and swaying tassels – signifying a new transitional phase in her evolution from child to woman. At the rear she wears an ntepana which is a smaller version of a married woman's rear apron. Like the foreskirt, it is usually adorned only with buttons and loose swinging vertical strings of beads similar to those found on the rear aprons of married women. **PAGES 152 AND 153:** The dwellings at Kwarrielaagte reflect the overall sense of community and solidarity among the Ntwana and the central role that women play as upholders of Ntwana custom. Their homesteads are microcosms of the larger community (kgoro) and represent the private world of the family within the broader social configuration. An Ntwana woman is entitled to her own homestead after the birth of her first child. On both the outer and inner main walls Ntwana women engage in mural decorations. Designs are sparse, minimalist and monochromatic, consisting of delicate geometric patterns or criss-cross motifs.

regarded as potential threats to the prosperity of the community. This ambivalence is highlighted by the relationship between women and cattle. Both are identified with and stand in opposition to one another. Both are symbols of fertility and both represent a threat to each other's procreative powers. For example, menstruating women are barred from the cattle enclosure. The reason for this is that, if a barren women enters the enclosure, an identical state will befall the cattle. Women are regarded as 'safe' only after menopause, when they discard all of their beaded waistbands, except for the lowest pink band. If pink is taken as representing a combination of red and white, the colour signifies sexual and, by implication, mystical neutrality.

This suggests that the Ntwana construct a very intricate, often ambivalent, relationship between particular colours, objects and the elements essential for their survival in both mystical and physical spheres. Colours are associated with states of heat and coolness, purity and danger, which serve to provide the Ntwana with a symbolic language that helps to make sense of a world which is often perceived as unintelligible, hostile and in a constant state of flux.

BELOW AND RIGHT: *The emphasis on Ntwana women as mothers and wives pervades their whole lives. Their modes of dress, the objects they produce and the rites they perform reinforce their role both as the upholders of custom and sustainers of the rural economy in the face of urbanization and in the absence of their menfolk, most of whom have been absorbed into the migrant labour force.*

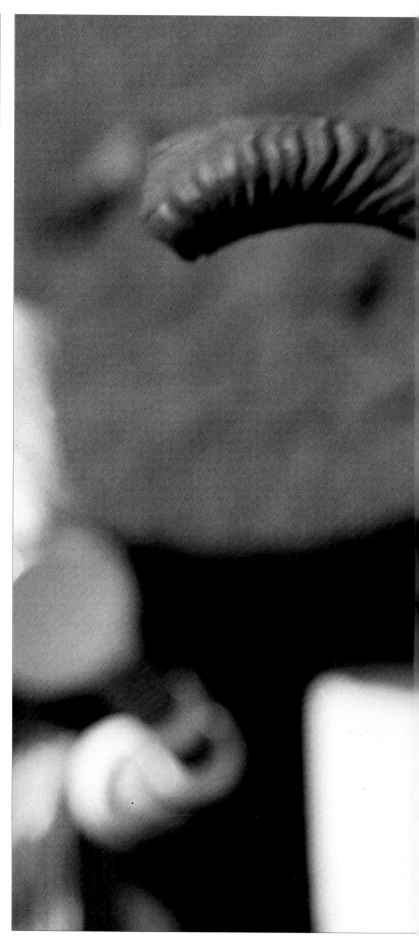

THE SAN

Ancestors of San-speakers were probably the earliest inhabitants of southern Africa,

with archaeological sites dating back hundreds of thousands of years. Sites from the

last 10,000 years of the Later Stone Age contain artefacts and evidence for practices

and ways of life which link them to historical and 20th-century San. Whether these

ancestors were also 'San' is unknown, as the word describes people speaking 'click'

languages within the Khoisan language group, and sites do not reveal languages.

The ancestors of the San lived mainly by gathering plants, hunting larger animals and trapping smaller game. At the coast, people also relied on food from the sea (fish, shell-fish and marine animals). They had no permanent settlements and travelled about the landscape according to their needs. Some 2,000 years ago, Khoekhoe people (herders who moved around with their sheep and cattle) and Iron Age farmers (who had livestock and cultivated crops, thus necessitating permanent settlements) migrated southwards into South Africa. From the Khoekhoe, to whom they were genetically and linguistically linked, San ancestors acquired the art of making pottery. Although they did not adopt the technology for making metal possessed by Iron Age farmers, metal artefacts in Later Stone Age sites show that there was also contact between hunter-gatherers and farmers. It seems that these peoples with different economies co-existed although, in pressurized colonial times, conflicts were recorded (for example, in the Drakensberg, where the San became experts at stealing cattle and horses from both black farmers and colonists). The demise of the southern San as a distinct cul-tural and economic group is perhaps due to the last few hundred years, and the impact of colonialism from the 17th century onward: San-speakers were enslaved, and in some instances exterminated *en masse*. Many others became labourers in and around colonial settlements and farms, which resulted in the destruction of the traditional identities of the southern San by the beginning of this century.

A belief that was prevalent for many years was that the San in the Kalahari Desert of Botswana and Namibia were descendants of fugitive people driven from better-watered parts of southern Africa. In fact, archaeological evidence reveals that the Kalahari has been occupied by hunter-gatherers for millennia. These peoples have been extensively studied by anthropologists and archaeologists, seeking parallels between modern hunter-gatherers and their ancestors. The San, how-ever, are not 'living fossils': like any other people they change with circumstances. Kalahari hunter-gatherers today retain many aspects of

ancient lifestyles, but are not isolated from the modern world and the money economy. Often marginalized, even today, they have adopted many strategies for economic, cultural and political sur-vival. For example, nowadays they may keep domestic animals (such as goats, donkeys and cattle) and have adopted aspects of a pastoralist (herding) way of life. The persistence of the San undoubtedly owes much to their rich and long-standing cultural traditions, which have helped them carve a niche in the arid Kalahari, with its minimal rainfall and extremes of temperature.

WAYS OF LIFE

At different times and places, San-speakers have lived in various ways; the Kalahari San are not necessary typical of all San and, even in the Kalahari groups, lifestyles may differ. Nevertheless, studies of Kalahari groups, for instance the Ju/'hoasi and the G/wi, create a general picture of the hunter-gatherer life. A division of labour between men and women is central to the economy. Plant foods are the dietary staple, and women, the chief gatherers, have expert knowledge of the veld: they know when and where resources such as melons, tubers, corms and berries are to be found. Women also collect or snare small fauna (such as reptiles, birds and small antelope). While out collecting, they

Top: Tobacco has long been an important and desirable trade commodity, and smoking is enjoyed by both men and women.
Opposite: A man plays the 'musical bow' or 'mouth bow', which was probably the forerunner of all string instruments. The mouth of the player serves as the resonator. Men may improvise tunes during their leisure time in the camp, or while they are walking in search of game.

THIS PAGE: A traditional dance, similar to the curing dance, where women clap and sing songs while men dance in a circle in a forward-bending posture. Anyone, even the very young, may participate. Here, the slaughter of a goat contributes to the celebration. *OPPOSITE:* The San successfully blend the old with the new: donkey-drawn carts may be made from parts of derelict vehicles; some people wear traditional clothing, but others have adopted a more Western dress style.

may observe the movements of the game and relay this information to the hunters. Men may gather food too, especially in the low hunting season. Gathered foods are distributed among the gatherer's family, while the larger game hunted by men is distributed among the whole group. The formidable reputation of the San as expert hunters is due to their outstanding tracking abilities and their ingenious hunting techniques. San trackers can follow spoor across virtually every land surface, even pursuing a wounded antelope among the spoor of a whole herd, until it finally leaves the herd and dies. Hunters use bows and arrows tipped with poison (derived from beetles or snakes) which does not contaminate the meat. However, it usually takes time before the poison works, allowing the dying animal to flee from its attackers, sometimes over considerable distances, making skilled tracking essential.

San arrows are clever instruments of death. Today, as in earlier times, they consist of four components. The point used to be made of bone or small skilfully flaked stones; today flattened nails or pieces of wire are used. The point is fitted into the 'link', which is tapered at either end and held in place by a reed collar. The link is fitted to the shaft in such a way that, when the arrow strikes its target, the impact breaks the link free from the shaft, reducing the likelihood of the head working loose, as there is less weight hanging from it. This also means that the animal cannot easily dislodge the point by rubbing against a tree. The poison is applied just behind the point, and the arrowhead has to stay in the animal for some time to ensure that the poison is adequately absorbed into the animal's system. The man who owns the arrow that killed the animal has the privilege of distributing the meat, according to rules of kinship, ensuring that everyone receives a portion. Sharing and the relative equality of all group members are important features of San societies. Though San groups did not have political chiefs, leadership was certainly recognized, according to seniority and ability. In traditional San societies, the husband went to live with the bride's parents on marriage. There were many rules of respect to be observed between the couple and their respective in-laws, whereas those separated by a generation (such as grandparents and grandchildren) were permitted a 'joking relationship', in which less formal conduct was appropriate. The San are known for their marked fondness for and indulgent attitude to children.

Typically, the group would split into smaller family units seasonally (usually when water and food were at their most sparse and dispersed), re-uniting at a later stage. Formalized gift giving, called *hxaro* by the Ju/'hoasi, is a way of maintaining reciprocal relationships between friends and relatives both in and beyond the group. This creates a web of support and access to resources over large areas. The importance of San kinship systems is echoed in religious beliefs, in myths and stories, and, obliquely, in the rock art.

RELIGION AND BELIEF

There is a great variety of beliefs among and even within different San groups, but there is also much held in common, even between vastly separated areas. In the late 19th century, a /Xam (Northern Cape San) man and another from Lesotho independently described their belief in a being named /Kaggen or Cagn. /Kaggen was a combined trickster and creator – powerful and sometimes benevolent, but capable of mischievous, malicious and stupid deeds. He was thought to have created the eland, the animal which appears most frequently in South African rock paintings. The Kalahari San have a similar trickster figure in their narrative traditions. The Ju/'hoasi described a great and a lesser god, the former associated with life and the rising sun, the latter with death and the west. A belief which was apparently ubiquitously held was that, when the world was first created, animals were indistinguishable

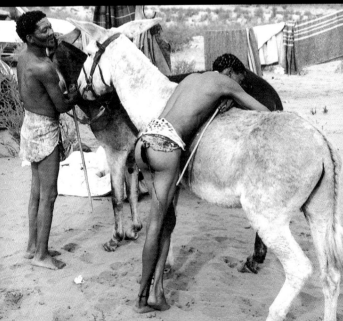

from the first people. These people had not yet acquired culture and manners. Only after a second creation were people and the animals separated, and people learnt how to observe a social code. Certain myths and stories, probably of great antiquity, are also very widely told.

Beliefs about death are less uniform. In the late 19th century, the same /Xam man explained that at death a person's heart went into the sky, where it became a star. Among recent Kalahari San too, a shooting star was associated with a person's death. Another southern San man described how a person's spirit or ghost walked from the grave to a 'great hole' underground, where dead people and animals lived. Most Kalahari groups seem to believe that the dead go to the great god's house in the sky. Northern and southern San believed that, even after death, people were capable of influencing the living. /Xam narrators described how people would speak to the dead to ask for help in hunting or bringing the rain. When shamans (healers) died, they were greatly feared and thought to be a particular danger to the living.

The ritual dances of the Kalahari San, where shamans enter a trance in order to cure the sick, are well known. A fire is lit, women start to clap and sing powerful medicine songs, and a dance which lasts all night begins. People initiated into the healing skills (both sexes) may go into a trance as a result of the rhythmic movement and music. It is believed that they have access to the lesser god who causes illness, and hence the ability to counteract the 'arrows of sickness' which he shoots into people. Trancers draw on a supernatural potency (num), believed to reside in various substances, including the sweat produced by the shaman's exertions. Another supernatural potency (n!ow) is linked to beliefs about birth, death and gender, and rain and weather. All humans and large herbivores possess n!ow. Humans acquire good

OPPOSITE: The San are known for their fondness for, and indulgent attitudes towards, children. These people migrated from the inner reaches of the Kalahari to their seasonal camp site in the semi-desert.
BELOW: The preparation and working of animal products are performed by men. From animals the San derive food, bone for artefacts, and leather for clothing. In the past, and still today, clothing was adorned with ostrich eggshell beads and buttons, but these days modern materials may be used. The decorations on this man's apron are reminiscent of the rock engravings with which the San are associated.

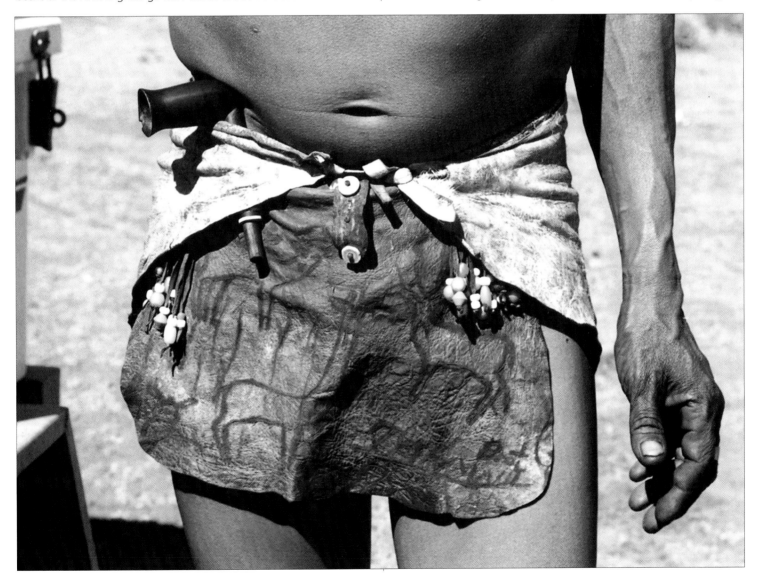

(rain-bringing) or bad (dry) *n!ow* at birth, and it is activated again at death. Rain-making was an important part of southern San religious belief and ritual. The /Xam of the Northern Cape (whose language and cultural unity no longer exist) described 'rain sorcerers', as well as 'game sorcerers' and 'sorcerers of illness' (healers). The religious beliefs known from many diverse San groups are currently thought to be crucial to understanding the rock art of southern Africa.

TREASURES OF THE CAVES

The spectacular paintings that the ancestors of the San left on the rocks and the walls of cave and shelter are arguably the most exquisite and finely detailed in the world's hunter-gatherer art. Equally skilled engravings (petroglyphs) are found principally in the interior of the country, but paintings occur more extensively, especially in rocky or mountainous areas such as the Drakensberg (KwaZulu-Natal), the Eastern Cape, and the south-western Cape (including the Cedarberg). Human figures and large antelope are by far most commonly depicted, and features of the landscape are rarely included. For unknown reasons, the engravings include more abstract designs than the paintings. Initially, many people thought that the art merely illustrated scenes from daily lives, or records of hunting, although the idea that the art was linked to religion and mythology was present from the start. The artistic tradition had died out by this century, and even earlier in some parts of the country.

The colours used by the San in their art were principally reds, from orange to brown and maroon; yellow; black and white; and their derivatives. Neither blue nor green was ever used. Sophisticated chemical techniques are needed to investigate the composition of the pigments, and many questions remain to be answered. Red pigments were obtained from haematite (red ochre) and yellows from limonite (yellow ochre). Manganese oxide and occasionally charcoal were used for black paints, while white pigment, which does not preserve well, may have been made from kaolin or bird droppings. In the 1930s, an old part-San man, who had observed San painters, demonstrated the process as he remembered it, and stated that he needed eland blood to mix with the pigment – undoubtedly a symbolic and magical ingredient.

Dating the rock art is extremely difficult. It cannot usually be carbon dated, because the pigments are inorganic (i.e. contain no carbon) and because the quantities of organic elements used are too small to test. If flakes of painted rock are found in archaeological deposits, organic material in the same layer can be dated, giving an approximate age. One Namibian site has yielded dates of over 26,000 years for slabs of rock with black pigment on them, but all other dates fall within the last 10,000 years. Most of the paintings still visible on the rock face are probably even younger, since the paint and rock surfaces are vulnerable to deterioration and decay. Drakensberg paintings of horses and soldiers indicate that these paintings cannot pre-date the 19th century.

A striking feature of San art is the stylized wide-striding human figures, which vividly depict action and speed. Action is shown in many different ways: dramatically, by animals galloping or leaping, and subtly,

BELOW: Rock paintings at the Stadsaal Caves (Cedarberg) are typical of the south-western Cape mountains. Rows of human figures are a feature of this area. Elephants are also often painted in this region, unlike the Drakensberg, where they are rarely portrayed.

by the flick of the tail or the twist of a neck. Sometimes the paintings create a sense of tension by capturing the moment just prior to action, such as an archer about to unleash his arrows, or a lion about to leap. Like other aspects of San life and culture, there is enormous variation and range, in style, subject matter and so forth, alongside similarities which suggest that they were inspired by similar religious beliefs. The fine bichrome (two colours) and polychrome (more than two colours) paintings of eland, an animal of great symbolic significance to the southern San, are one pointer to the religious affiliation of some, perhaps most, of the art. Paintings of dances, where women clap while men dance, also link some of the art to ritual healing, as known from the Kalahari San. Paintings of soldiers, wagons, and similar imagery may have been partly magical in function, but also record historical events – including those which led ultimately to the termination of the painting tradition, and the San hunter-gatherer way of life in South Africa.

ABOVE: *The unity of San family groups can be seen in this touching portrait of a mother and son.* **PAGE 164, TOP:** *Hunter-gatherers, since they move in search of natural resources, do not make permanent structures. Branches and grasses form windbreaks (skerms), which are commonly erected in a roughly circular arrangement, around a central hearth. When the group moves on, the shelter is left to disintegrate.* **PAGE 164, BOTTOM:** *The elderly are highly respected and cared for, but traditionally an old person, who was unable to keep up with a band that was on the move, might be left behind in the veld with food and water; if a new camp site were soon found, he or she would be fetched. Necessity dictated that the ailing be left to their fate, rather than threaten the survival of the entire group.* **PAGE 165:** *Children and grandparents have a close bond, and enjoy an informal relationship that is not permitted between parents and their children, or a couple and their in-laws.*

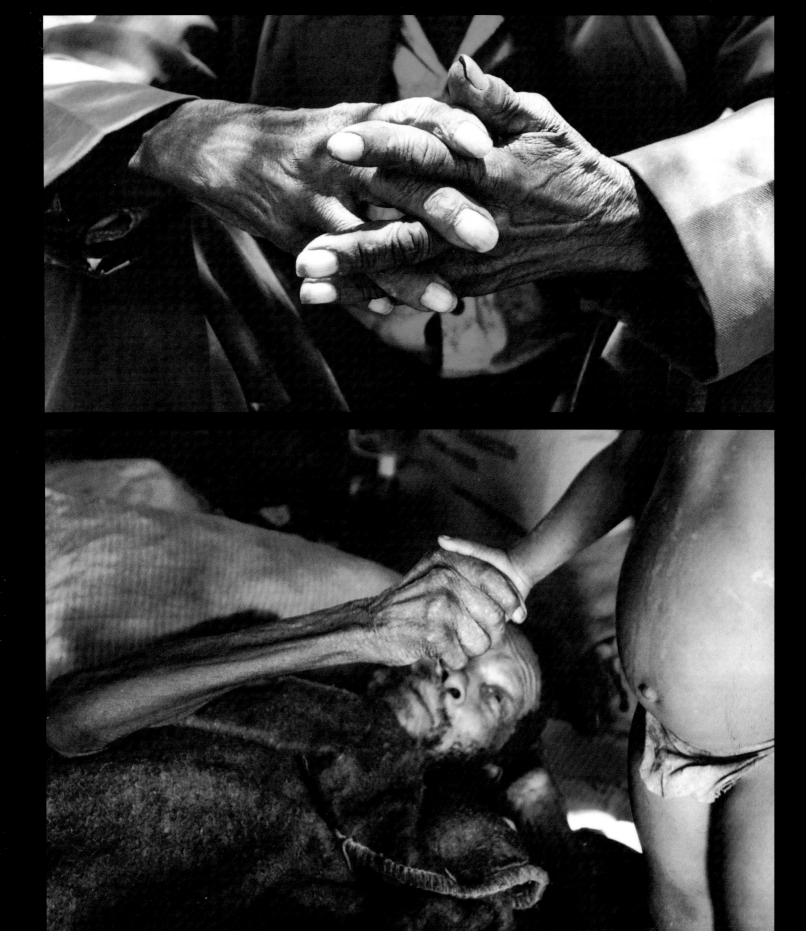

INDEX

Page numbers in *italic* refer to photographs and maps; those in **bold** indicate main entries.

FURTHER READING

Alverson, Hoyt (1978) *Mind in the Heart of Darkness.* Yale University Press, New Haven.

Cameron, T. and Spies, S.B. (eds) (1991) *A New Illustrated History of South Africa* (second edition), Southern Books Publishers, Johannesburg, and Human & Rousseau, Cape Town.

Comaroff, Jean (1985) *Body of Power, Spirit of Resistance.* Chicago University Press, Chicago.

Comaroff, Jean and Comaroff, John (1991) *Of Revelation and Revolution.* Chicago University Press, Chicago.

Comaroff, John and Roberts, Simon (1981) *Rules and Processes.* Chicago University Press, Chicago.

Coplan, David (1996) *In the Time of Cannibals.* Chicago University Press, Chicago.

Davison, P. et al (1991) *Art and Ambiguity: Perspectives on the Brenthurst Collection of Southern African Art.* Johannesburg Art Gallery Collection of Essays, Johannesburg.

Delius, P. (1983) *The Land Belongs to Us: The Pedi Polity, the Boers and the British in the Nineteenth-Century Transvaal.* Ravan Press, Johannesburg.

Delius, P. (1989) 'The Ndzundza Ndebele' in Bonner, P., Hofmeyr, I., James, D., and Lodge, T. (eds), *Holding their Ground: Class, Locality and Culture in 19th and 20th Century South Africa.* Ravan Press, Johannesburg.

Delius, P. (1996) *A Lion Amongst the Cattle: Reconstruction and Resistance in the Northern Transvaal.* Ravan Press, Johannesburg.

Duminy, A. and Guest, B. (eds) (1989) *Natal and Zululand. From Earliest Times to 1910. A New History.* University of Natal Press and Shuter and Shooter, Pietermaritzburg.

Eldredge, Elizabeth (1993) *A South African Kingdom.* Cambridge University Press, Cambridge.

Ferguson, James (1990) *The Anti-Politics Machine.* Cambridge University Press, Cambridge.

Hall, M. (1987) *The Changing Past: Farmers, Kings and Traders in Southern Africa, 200–1860.* David Philip, Cape Town.

Hammond-Tooke, W.D. (ed.) (1980) *The Bantu-Speaking Peoples of Southern Africa.* Routledge and Kegan Paul, London.

Harries, Patrick (1994) *Work, Culture and Identity: Migrant Labourers in Mozambique and South Africa, c. 1860–1910.* Heinemann, Portsmouth N.H., James Currey, London, and Witwatersrand University Press, Johannesburg.

James, D. (1994) *Mmino wa setšo: Songs of Town and Country and the Experience of Migrancy by Men and Women from the Northern Transvaal.* University of the Witwatersrand, Johannesburg.

Lye, William and Murray, Colin (1980) *Transformations on the Highveld.* David Philip, Cape Town.

Maclennan, B. (1986) *A Proper Degree of Terror: John Graham and the Cape's Eastern Frontier.* Ravan Press, Johannesburg.

Maylam, P. (1986) *A History of the African People of South Africa: From the Early Iron Age to the 1970s.* David Philip, Cape Town.

Peires, J.B. (1989) *The Dead will Arise: Nongqause and the Great Cattle-Killing Movement of 1856–7.* Ravan Press, Johannesburg.

Saunders, C. (ed.) (1988) *Reader's Digest Illustrated History of South Africa: The Real Story.* Reader's Digest, Cape Town.

Shostak, M. (1983) *Nisa: The Life and Words of a !Kung Woman.* Penguin, Harmondsworth.

Skotnes, P. (ed.) (1996) *Miscast: Negotiating the Presence of the Bushmen.* University of Cape Town Press, Cape Town.

Van Vuuren, C.J. (1995) 'Ndebele' in Middelton, J. and Assam, R. (eds), *Encyclopedia of World Cultures, Vol. 9.* G.K. Hall, Boston.

Wilson, M. and Thompson, L. (eds) (1982) *A History of South Africa to 1870.* David Philip, Cape Town.